San Diego, California

Signing Naturally Student Workbook, Units 1–6.
Copyright © 2008 Smith, Lentz, Mikos,
All Rights Reserved.

Published by DawnSignPress

ISBN: 978-1-58121-210-5

Printed in China

10 9 8 7 6 5 4 3

ATTENTION

Quantity discounts and special
purchase arrangements available for teachers

DAWN**S**IGN**P**RESS
6130 Nancy Ridge Drive
San Diego, CA 92121-3223
(858) 625-0600 V • (858) 625-2336 FAX
(858) 768-0478 VP
Visit us at www.dawnsign.com

SIGNING NATURALLY

Table of Contents

WITHDRAWN

Photo Credits

COLORS #1 by Chuck Baird.
Photo courtesy of DawnSignPress (p. 1).

FIELD OF POPPIES by Granville R. S. Redmond.
Photo courtesy of California School for the Deaf, Fremont (p. 45).

HEARING IMPAIRED: wrong way/DEAF: right way.
© 1992, Ann Silver.
Courtesy of the artist (p. 175).

BUY ME! I KNOW SIGN LANGUAGE by Shawn Richardson.
Photo courtesy of the artist (p. 229).

Deaf Profiles:

Andrew Foster.
Courtesy of Gallaudet University Archives, Washington, DC. (p. 14).

Regina Olson Hughes.
Courtesy of Gallaudet University Archives, Washington, DC. (p. 70).

Douglas Tilden.
Courtesy of Gallaudet University Archives, Washington, DC. (p. 113).

Marie Philip.
Courtesy of The Learning Center, Boston, Massachusetts. (p. 186).

Clayton Valli.
Courtesy of DawnSignPress. (p. 276).

Introduction

The Signing Naturally Units 1-6 Student Workbook and DVDs are designed to compliment course work in American Sign Language (ASL). These introductory materials, along with class instruction, give you basic vocabulary, grammar, and expressive practice to develop your everyday conversational skills in ASL.

This introduction will cover information about what to expect in the classroom, provide brief information about ASL, Deaf Culture, and the Deaf community, review the materials, and tell you how to prepare for class.

You're Taking an ASL Class!

Since you've enrolled in this course, you probably already have an interest in ASL. Maybe you've seen an interpreter at a performance or in a classroom. Or you've met a Deaf person, have a Deaf family member, friend or neighbor. Now that you've decided to learn ASL, be prepared to open your mind to a new language and culture.

Human communication is really a set of symbols (this applies to signs, sounds and printed pictures or words) that users agree have the same meaning. For ASL, an obvious difference from spoken language is the *modality*, which for ASL is visual and gestural. Students of ASL can expect to acquire many insights, not only into the universal aspects common to all languages, but also specific information that is found in studying ASL and learning about its community of users.

A Brief History of ASL

For over 250 years, ASL has evolved in the U.S. and Canada as the means for Deaf people to express and share their ideas, needs and thoughts. Although it is primarily Deaf people who use ASL, hearing people around them acquire and use the language also. They are children born to Deaf parents, siblings of Deaf children, other family members, neighbors, friends, co-workers, supervisors or employees of Deaf people. Since the mid-1960s when linguists recognized ASL as a distinct language (something that was true all along, but only "discovered in the 1960s), a growing number of hearing people have elected to learn ASL in major colleges, universities, and high schools throughout the country.

The origins of ASL can be traced to a couple of major historical influences. There is evidence that in the 1600s some of the inhabitants of Martha's Vineyard off Cape Cod had a genetic pool that resulted in a large number of Deaf people in the community. This in turn resulted in naturally formed signing communities on the island. Likewise, on the mainland, various indigenous signs were used where Deaf people were members of villages. These regional sign languages were brought by the students to the first school for the Deaf founded in Hartford, Connecticut, in 1817.

The second major influence was French Sign Language, brought by the school's founders, Laurent Clerc, a Deaf teacher from France, and Thomas Gallaudet, a hearing American minister. The blending of the indigenous sign language and French sign language formed the basis for ASL today.

Similar to other language minority groups within the U.S., it is common for the native language to be acquired within the family. This process is true for only 8-10% of Deaf children who are born into families with Deaf members. A larger percentage of Deaf children, around 70%, are raised in hearing families that do not sign. The remaining 20% of Deaf children have hearing families who use ASL and embrace Deaf culture. For Deaf children, the Deaf residential school has been the primary venue for learning ASL. The constant exposure to signing Deaf peers, Deaf teachers and dorm counselors has made it possible for the children to develop fluency in the language.

Bilingual Education and Oralism

The early 19th century saw ASL flourish through residential schools, which had immense success in Deaf education utilizing ASL and written English. Gallaudet University was founded in 1864 with a charter signed by President Abraham Lincoln. Gallaudet University was (and still is) a bastion for using signing in higher education as well as contributing to the standardization ASL among Deaf people in other states where many graduates returned home to teach.

From there, highly evolved Deaf signing communities formed complex networks all across the country. The communities maintained constant contact through organized sports, conferences, social and political events, and the arts.

However, a pivotal moment in ASL and Deaf America's history occurred in 1880, with repercussions that are still being felt today. At the International Congress on the Education of the Deaf Conference in Milan, Italy, educators who supported oral instruction for Deaf students successfully blocked the influence of educators supporting Sign language. The congress voted in favor or oral education for all Deaf children. In a span of 40 years following the conference, the percentage of Deaf children being taught by the oral method grew from a very small percentage to an astounding 80%. Before that, Deaf teachers constituted 45% of all teachers of the Deaf, but that figure went down to only 11%. In many parts of Europe, Deaf teachers were dismissed because they were unable to teach speech. The oral approach to Deaf education became a contentious issue for the next century and a half, reflecting the broader society's misplaced belief that spoken language is superior to sign language.

Fortunately, during that time, Deaf children lived most of the year at schools. Despite not understanding much of what went on in the classroom, after school, in the dormitory and on the playing fields, ASL was still used to exchange information, to share understandings and learn other life lessons. Generally, at best, ASL was tolerated by the staff in the dormitories. This approach (banning signing in the classroom, and tolerating it outside the classroom) took its toll on the general Deaf community. Deaf people's perception of ASL and themselves as capable human beings diminished drastically. Confidence and pride waned as the quality of education declined for Deaf people. What carried them through those years was the ability to continue networking with each other at the Deaf clubs, Gallaudet University, and other social events.

The 1960s and Onward

In the 1960s, linguists at Gallaudet University proved that ASL is a fully developed independent language unrelated to English. From there, a resurgence of a positive view of ASL and Deaf culture empowered Deaf people to reclaim control of the institutions that impact their lives. In 1988, when the Board of Trustees at Gallaudet University selected a hearing president who didn't know ASL, the students staged a weeklong protest and succeeded in appointing the first Deaf president of the university.

Interestingly, while Deaf people have struggled for decades to bring ASL back to the classroom as the language of instruction in Deaf education, ASL enjoys tremendous popularity among hearing parents and their babies. Literature shows that learning signs early in infancy has a positive effect on general language development and enhances the parent–child relationship. Studies further show that signing babies understand more words, have a larger vocabulary and engage in more sophisticated play than non-signing babies. Yet the language has not been systematically made available to many Deaf babies.

Issues surrounding ASL and Deaf education continue to be contentious, but the resiliency of ASL in the face of many obstacles is a testament to its value in meeting the powerful human need for communication.

A Brief Introduction to Deaf Culture

There are two popular uses of the word culture. One means to have a sophisticated taste or to be well read, appreciate art, literature, cuisine—to be cultured. The other use of culture relates to the unique attributes of a certain group of people. Various groups of people develop distinctive ways of describing, valuing, and behaving in the world. This is their culture. Anthropologists have been formally studying world cultures for years, and mindful people have been pondering and examining culture as long as human societies have existed. Yet, having a deep understanding of culture still can be elusive.

One way of understanding a culture is to look at how the members identify themselves. Over the years different terms have been used to refer to Deaf people. Some older terms are considered offensive today and should not be used, especially "deaf and dumb" and "deaf mute." The terms "hearing impaired," "deaf and hard of hearing," or "people with hearing loss" have been used by public institutions, political groups, and some individuals, as an attempt to be inclusive, but those terms focus on what is perceived as lacking or lost. The term "Deaf" with a capital "D" is an inclusive term because it focuses on what people *have*—a living culture, an available language, and the infinite, untapped possibilities being Deaf can offer.

People within Deaf culture value being kept informed about the environment, the community, and its members. Since the majority culture's primary ways of disseminating information are not visually centered, Deaf people are expected to have a sense of social obligation and duty to others within Deaf culture. This includes sharing information and offering updates on what is going on in the Deaf world as well as the broader world. In fulfilling this duty to the group, one tends to develop long-term relationships and complex networking systems. Similar to more than 70% of cultures in the world (many found in Africa, Asia and Latin America), in Deaf culture the group comes before the individual. Although the Deaf community recognizes individual achievements and talents, contributing to the group's success is very highly valued. This is different than in American culture where great emphasis is placed on independence, self-reliance, achievement and individual success.

One visible cultural behavior among Deaf signers is how their eyes are used during signed interactions. For example, while watching another person sign, they would focus on the signer's face, while reading the signs within their peripheral vision. This is to get valuable information about the grammar of the sentence which is shown simultaneously on the face.

Another visible cultural behavior among Deaf signers is how they get other people's attention. Examples are waving in others' peripheral vision, tapping on certain parts of the body and/or hitting a surface to create vibrations.

Yet another visible cultural behavior is how Deaf people locate themselves and move among people in signing situations. For example, if a path is blocked by two signers conversing, the Deaf person does not wait until the signers stop talking, bend down to pass, or find another path, but just walks through.

It's considered rude when one watches a signed conversation in public and not inform the signers you know ASL. Additionally, a person who knows ASL and chooses to speak without signing in front of Deaf people can be considered disrespectful and insensitive to Deaf people.

Throughout this book there are examples of cultural behavior typical in the Deaf community. Since the concept of culture is complex, it may take time and personal experience to identify the distinctive qualities of Deaf culture and more fully understand them. Until you have more exposure to and connection with Deaf culture, it is best to have an open mind, be respectful, and enjoy the uniqueness of Deaf culture and the challenge and fun of using ASL.

Debunking Some Myths about ASL

Probably the most important myth to debunk is that ASL is not a visual code for English, written or spoken. The differences are significant. ASL and English use different modalities (visual/gesture/ as opposed to aural/oral), and have different phonology and grammar. For new students, it is important to avoid reliance on English syntax and usage while signing, since this will result in a poor command of ASL.

Another common myth to debunk is that ASL is a language of pictures and pantomime. If true, nobody would have problems understanding ASL! Although some signs in ASL appear to have features similar to actual things or actions, most ASL signs do not.

Another myth to debunk is that ASL is a universal language understood by all signers in the world. In fact, there are hundreds of identified sign languages in the world, most of them developed indigenously by Deaf people in their countries.

What to Expect in the Classroom

All communication in the classroom will be in ASL. This approach, which immerses you in the language, is the best way to become comfortable with the language, retain what you've learned, and improve both your *receptive* and *expressive* skills.

There are no English equivalents in this workbook. That means, while there are some signs that have a brief description in English to help you grasp the meaning, avoid "assigning" the meaning of an English word to an ASL sign. Many ASL signs simply are not directly translatable to English words. So if you develop a habit of seeing ASL signs and doing a mental run through of English, you will often make wrong sign choices. ASL signs are best learned through use and context.

Often students are tempted to hold on to the crutch of English by speaking while signing. This is not a good idea. Trying to speak and sign results in bad ASL syntax and grammar. The faster you can develop a complete reliance on ASL only when signing, the more quickly you will progress.

The classroom most likely will be set up so all students sit in a semi-circle so that every one can see each other. Visually based language relies on people being able to see each other to see what is being signed. Watching every conversation, sign, and exchange will benefit your own language skills.

STUDENT MATERIALS

Student Workbook

The Student Workbook is used in the classroom, and also used outside the class, along with the Student DVDs, for additional study, review, and practice. The workbook is important and should be brought to each class. The workbook has several sections:

- **Homework**

  Homework is numbered by Unit, and corresponds with a lesson learned in class. For example, Homework 1.1 corresponds to your first lesson from Unit 1. The teacher will tell you which homework to complete after each class. Homework is mostly video-related and each homework section has instructions for you to follow.

- **Vocabulary Review**

  Each unit has a vocabulary review section that includes important signs from the lesson and your homework. The video captures on the page have corresponding video for you to watch, study and practice.

- **Classroom Exercises**

  These exercises are used in the classroom as part of the lesson. The exercises are developed specifically to provide the opportunity to use grammatical feature(s) and rehearse new vocabulary you learned during the lesson. Your teacher will tell you when to open your workbooks to these pages.

- **Video Captures**

  The printed video captures are a reference to the clip on the video for that sign or phrase. Studying the video will always be a better way to review signs, but the printed video captures also have arrows added to show motion.

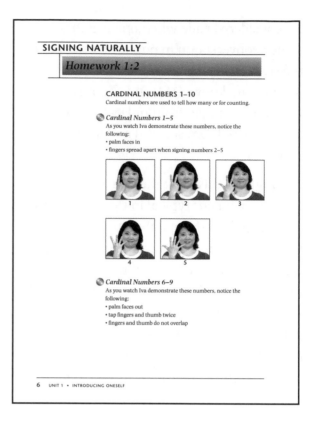

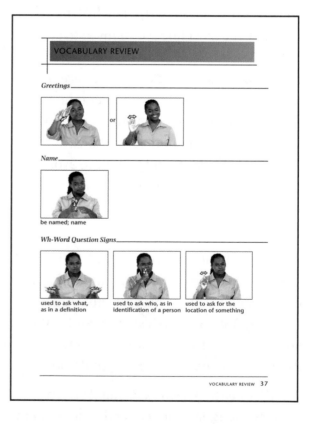

The basic five parameters of every sign are handshape, palm orientation, location, movement, and "non-manual" features such as facial expressions. When evaluating a video capture to study a sign, first identify how each of these elements contributes to the sign.

Because ASL is a visually active language the most difficult requirement of a sign illustration is to show movement. To facilitate the three-dimensional nature of signs, illustrations incorporate a number of helpful features.

Arrows show the direction, path, and repetition of the movement. Here are the arrows you will see.

- **Directional arrows** point in the direction the sign is to be made.

- **Bi-directional** arrows indicate a back and forth motion.

- **Path arrows** show you the path of the sign's movement.

- **Repetitive arrows** indicate that the sign's movement repeats twice or more.

A touch is when part of the sign touches the chest, shoulder, or other part of the body. Touches are shown with touch marks.

When a sign is supposed to be "wiggled" or moved back and forth slightly, there will be wiggle marks indicating this. Here are examples of wiggle marks.

The video captures in this book are meant only as a reference point to the DVD. The DVD is the main source of information about the signs, and you should use it as the primary source of information about the signs included in this book.

You will also see video captures in a rounded box, these do not have a corresponding clip on the DVDs. Those captures look like this.

The Student DVDs

The Student DVDs contain video clips that correspond to homework in the workbook. Vocabulary Review sections help you study the signs in a "stand alone" way, outside of a dialogue.

There are two DVDs, disk one, and disk two. Disk one contains the video material for Units 1–3, and disk two contains the video material for Units 4–6.

The main menu of the DVD looks like this.

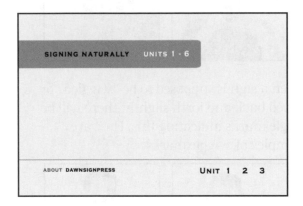

After you select a Unit, a Homework menu appears so you can choose the homework section you want to study. For the Vocabulary Review of that unit, you will see VR. Select that to study the vocabulary for the unit.

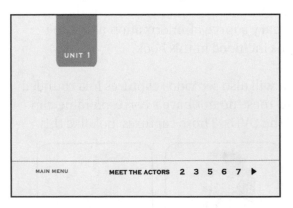

As video clips play, the "navigation bar" remains on the screen, indicating which unit and homework you are watching (see the close up below). For example, if the number shows 1:2, it means you are watching Homework 1 from Unit 2.

At the end of video clips that require you to write, draw, or answer, two symbols appear that allow you to play the section again, or move on to the next numbered question.

After you have watched all of the video clips for a specific homework, the DVD brings you back to the homework menu so you can choose which clips to watch next.

Remember these things when using the DVDs:

1. All of the instructions for how to use the video to complete your homework appear in the workbook. Read all instructions in the workbook before starting any activity.

2. The DVDs are designed for you to complete the homework section in one sitting. If you need to skip forward in the DVD, use your remote control or DVD controls on your computer. The video must be playing to skip forward, you can't skip forward through the numbered sections of the DVD unless the video is playing.

The signers in the Student DVDs are identified by their actual names in the workbook, unless they are acting out a story or dialogue using another name. You can "meet" the actors by playing the section on the Unit 1 menu.

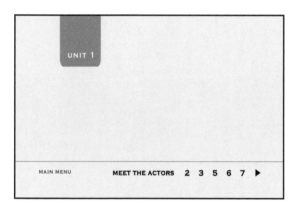

Unit 6

Unit 6 is a storytelling unit. The goal of Unit 6 is to help you develop your narrative skills in ASL. Your teacher will decide when to assign homework from this unit, and it may be that homework from this unit is assigned alongside homework from other units as you progress through the class.

How to Prepare for Class

The amount of time you spend using ASL outside of class will greatly increase your ability to retain new vocabulary. One easy way to help remember what you learned in class is to do your homework as soon as you can. In a single day a person can lose up to 40% of what they have learned!

It is also helpful to form study groups with other classmates. Even if you come to class 10 minutes early and converse in ASL with others, it will be a good reinforcement of what you've learned.

Things to Remember as You Learn ASL

Why no English?

Often new students wonder why there are no English words offered as "equivalents" to ASL signs. There is a concept in language learning called *linguistic interference*. This happens when one language's structure, meaning, and vocabulary hinders language students' ability to engage with the second language on its own. It can be tempting to try and find English words that "match" signs. But it is best to leave English outside the classroom, and it has intentionally been separated from ASL signs in the book and videos.

In this introductory set of materials, basic meanings of signs are used, as is appropriate for new students. There are often many other nuances and meanings for signs that are not possible to cover in an introductory course. Please do not limit your understanding of an ASL sign by thinking there is a one-to-one correspondence to English words.

Another type of linguistic interference happens when you try to sign and speak at the same time. If you try this, your first language will most likely supercede the correct grammar for ASL, and often result in using the wrong signs to express what you want to say.

Both ASL and English are natural languages that can express anything, but they are also separate languages. Try to begin to think in ASL, matching concepts to signs. Your study of the language will benefit greatly.

Please Don't Speak in Class

Even if you think whispering to your neighbor will not disrupt the classroom, remember that to listen in ASL means you are looking at the person signing and giving them your full attention. If you are talking in class, you not only interrupt your own learning, but you take others attention away from what is being taught. If you must get another person's attention, please use behaviors appropriate to a visual, signing environment (see page 33 for information about this topic).

Relax and Have Fun!

As is true for all language courses that rely on immersion techniques, you may feel lost or unsure at times. But remember that the more you express yourself and learn to understand other signers, your progress with ASL will be smoother and more enjoyable.

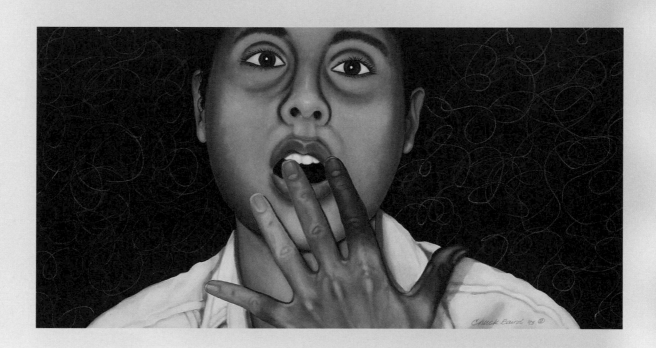

Colors #1 Chuck Baird

Signing "color," a model's outspread
hand, with each finger a different shade,
is held to her mouth.

-L. K. Elion, *Chuck Baird: 35 Plates*

UNIT 1

Introducing Oneself

Homework 1:1

STRATEGIES FOR LEARNING AMERICAN SIGN LANGUAGE (ASL)

To increase your language learning in the classroom, develop the following habits:

1. **Build a language community.**

   Try not to miss class, especially at the beginning. Your class strives to form a language community: the cohesiveness of the group influences how rich the language exchange is in the classroom. Missing class makes it difficult to achieve this interactive environment. Maintain a signing environment in the classroom, during class breaks, before class begins, and whenever Deaf people are present.

2. **Minimize reliance on English as you listen or converse in ASL.**

   Leave English (and your voice) outside the door. Try not to translate in your head as you watch someone sign. At first, this will be difficult to do but as you become more fluent, the temptation should lessen. Do not worry about taking notes during class. Instead use class time to immerse yourself in the language by interacting with the teacher and other students using ASL. The student DVD and workbook will help you retain the language introduced in class.

3. **Focus on meaning rather than individual signs.**

   When your teacher tells a story, gives instructions, or explains a concept, try not to worry about a sign you missed or don't know. Instead, focus on the meaning of what's being said. If a particular sign is repeated over and over, and you still can't figure out its meaning, then ask the teacher. Try to avoid asking your classmates for an English translation. You would lose out on valuable communication experiences needed to strengthen your comprehension skills.

4. Focus on the signer's face, not on the hands for two very important reasons.

First, a lot of grammar is in the facial expression so to really know what is said, you must see both the facial expression and what is signed; secondly, it is considered rude to look away from the signers' face while they are signing to you.

5. Show you understand the signer.

Nod to show you are following along; give a puzzled look when you are not. Develop active listening behaviors like nodding, responding with the signs "huh?" "wow," or "really?" Listeners have very active roles in signed conversations. Actively listening increases your comprehension skills and optimizes your learning. Participate as much as possible by adding comments, agreeing or disagreeing, etc. Follow all conversations whether they are between teacher and class, teacher and student, or student and student. The more you participate, the more you will retain what you learn.

Assignment

• Choose a strategy you will work on for the next month.
• Write down the number and explain why you chose that strategy.
• Submit the paper next class.

Homework 1:2

CARDINAL NUMBERS 1–10

Cardinal numbers are used to tell how many or for counting.

💿 *Cardinal Numbers 1–5*

As you watch Iva demonstrate these numbers, notice the following:
- palm faces in
- fingers spread apart when signing numbers 2–5

1

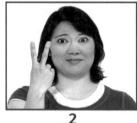
2

3

4

5

💿 *Cardinal Numbers 6–9*

As you watch Iva demonstrate these numbers, notice the following:
- palm faces out
- tap fingers and thumb twice
- fingers and thumb do not overlap

6

7

8

9

10

Cardinal Number 10

As you watch Iva demonstrate this number, notice the following:
• extend thumb upward
• slightly rock hand back and forth

Sign the Numbers

Now you count from 1 to 10. Try to sign the number before Joey, then check to see if you've signed it correctly!

Circle the Number

Numbers 3, 6 and 9, and 7 and 8, are often confused for each other. Practice recognizing these numbers.

Circle the number signed:

1.	3	6	9
2.	7	8	9
3.	3	6	9
4.	7	8	9
5.	3	6	9
6.	7	8	9

Answers on page 397.

Write the Number

Now write down the number signed.

1. _____   6. _____

2. _____   7. _____

3. _____   8. _____

4. _____   9. _____

5. _____   10. _____

Answers are given in class.

Homework 1:3

FINGERSPELLING NAMES

In the Deaf community, you introduce yourself by fingerspelling your name. Fingerspelling is a skill that requires a lot of practice to become proficient. Here are a few insider tips—learn them well and you'll be on your way.

Fingerspelling Flow

When you fingerspell a word, work on the continuous flow of one letter to the next, rather than spelling the word letter by letter. Avoid "bouncing" or "stamping" the letters as you spell.

Arm Position

Keep your elbow down and your arm relaxed.

incorrect

correct

Hand Position 1: Fingerspelling to Person in Front

When you fingerspell words to someone in front of you, be sure to keep your hand within what we call the "sightline"—the visual space between your face and your listener's face. Your hand should be in front of your chin or slightly below. This way your listener can easily see both your face and your hand.

incorrect

correct

Hand Position 2: Fingerspelling to Person Next to You

When you fingerspell to a person on either side of you, orient your hand toward the person and within the sightline.

To a person on your non-dominant side

incorrect

correct

To a person on your dominant side

incorrect

correct

⊙ Hand Position 3: Fingerspelling to Someone above You

When you sit and fingerspell to a person who is standing, move your hand up to face the listener within the sightline.

incorrect   correct

Reading Fingerspelling

Reading someone's fingerspelling is not easy. It takes time to develop the skill. Everyone approaches fingerspelling differently. But all agree that it takes practice, practice, and more practice. Here are a few suggestions.

• work on recognizing the shape and the movement of letters and letter combinations. Begin with names of your classmates. Pick out two or three students at a time and learn to recognize their name when the teacher does the roll call. Continue adding two or three more names, until you can recognize everyone's name.

• work on catching the first and last letters of the word and use context (what is being discussed) to help you guess the word spelled.

• don't be timid. Ask the person to spell the word again and again—until you understand the word. Keep a list of words you have trouble with and ask a study buddy to spell the list to you.

FIST LETTERS

The manual alphabet is handshapes associated with the 26 letters in the English alphabet. You will learn more about how and when to use those handshapes throughout this workbook. We begin with practicing the "fist" letters here, which include the following letters—**A E I O S T M N.**

For all these letters, the thumb is an important element in forming the letters correctly. Pay attention to the thumb position.

 View. Cinnie demonstrates the dos and don'ts of forming the "fist" letters.

The letter "A"
The thumb is straight up flush to the hand.
Do not bend thumb over the fingers. The fingers are not tucked in.

The letter "E"
At least two fingers must sit on the thumb.
Do not have the thumb overlap the fingers.

The letter "I"
The thumb curves over the index finger and stays tight to the fist.

The letter "O"
Do not make a perfectly round "O" shape, instead make a relaxed "oval-shaped O."

The letter "S"
This is the "true fist." Fingers are tucked in and the thumb straps over the index and middle fingers.

The letter "T"
Relax the index finger that crosses over the thumb. The index finger does not have to curl down tightly. The other fingers are not tucked in.

The letters "N" and "M"
The fingers sit softly on the thumb.

🔘 Practice
On the DVD, Tyrone demonstrates these letter combinations. Practice copying until you feel comfortable.

> **NOTE:** A chart illustrating all 26 letters of the alphabet can be found on pages 19–20.

1.	am	an	at
2.	ea	en	es
3.	ma	mo	mi
4.	na	ne	no
5.	oe	on	is
6.	sa	se	st
7.	ta	te	to
8.	en	es	ie
9.	im	mo	me
10.	ne	no	ni

⊙ Circle the Letter

Watch Tyrone and circle the letter combination given.

1.	ae	ao	as
2.	sa	so	se
3.	sn	st	sm
4.	mi	ni	ti
5.	mi	ei	si
6.	ei	ie	ai
7.	en	on	sn
8.	ta	sa	na
9.	oe	os	oa
10.	ea	oa	os

Answers on page 397.

⊙ Circle the Letter 2

Watch Tyrone and circle the letter combination given.

1.	ae	ao	as
2.	sa	so	se
3.	sn	st	sm
4.	mi	ni	ti
5.	mi	ei	si
6.	ei	ie	ai
7.	en	on	sn
8.	ta	oa	na
9.	oe	os	oa
10.	ea	oa	os

Answers are given in class.

DEAF PROFILE

ANDREW FOSTER (1925-1987)

Andrew J. Foster spent his life dedicated to improving education for Deaf people. A teacher, pioneer, and missionary, his legacy lives on in the many schools he opened in West Africa.

Foster was born in a steel-mill town near Birmingham, Alabama and attended the Alabama School for the Colored Deaf in Talladega after losing his hearing at the age of 11. At the Alabama school, he learned ASL and became a life-long proponent of the language. At 17, Foster moved to Michigan, taking night classes and working odd jobs. He was accepted at Gallaudet University in 1951 as one of the first of three Black Deaf students to be enrolled at the school.

While attending Gallaudet Foster saw an address book of world Deaf schools, which listed only 12 in Africa. Foster felt called to service, writing that he was "moved by this vast educational and spiritual void among my people." He received his Bachelor's Degree in 1954, and in the next two years received a Masters degree from Eastern Michigan University, and a second Masters from Seattle Pacific Christian College.

He was deeply determined to help Deaf people in Africa, but struggling to find help for his mission, he founded the Christian Mission for the Deaf (CMD) in 1956. He went to Africa in 1957. Within a year, he had established the first school for the Deaf in Accra, Ghana in a small room borrowed from a church. Twelve students attended the first year. The school quickly grew to 53 Deaf students. Children met from 4 to 5 in the afternoon, and adults met from 6-7 in the evening. By 1959 the school had a waiting list of over 100, and in five years, the waiting list was over 300.

In the following years, Foster continued his life's work, opening schools for the Deaf all over West Africa. He went to Nigeria and opened three more schools before 1962. In all, he established 31 schools for the Deaf in thirteen countries including Ghana, Benin,

> *"Employing restrictive and suppressive means of communication to achieve normalcy seems as illogical as it is impractical."*

> *Foster believed that freedom of communication was the key to education, and that freedom was achieved through sign language.*

Congo, Chad, Ivory Coast, Kenya, Nigeria, Sierra Leone, and Cameroon. He also founded the African Bible College for the Deaf and became the President of the Council for the Education and Welfare of the Deaf in Africa. The schools used sign language, becoming oases of communication for Deaf people. In recognition of his amazing achievements, Gallaudet University awarded him the Honorary Doctorate in 1970.

A staunch supporter of educating Deaf children through sign language, Foster said in his 1975 keynote speech at the World Federation of the Deaf conference in Washington DC, "Employing restrictive and suppressive means of communication to achieve normalcy seems as illogical as it is impractical." Foster believed that freedom of communication was the key to education, and that freedom was achieved through sign language.

He spent years training teachers in Africa, offering intensive teaching courses new teachers could go on to set up schools of their own. By 1974, there were 70 Deaf schools in Africa. Continuing his training through the 80s, Foster also continued traveling the world speaking and fundraising for his cause, touching 47 of the 50 U.S. states, speaking throughout Europe and traveling to 25 African countries. In 1987 Foster died at the age of 62 in a plane crash in Rwanda and was buried there.

His inspiring life is evident in the many ways his memory is honored. The National Association of the Deaf's Andrew J. Foster Award recognizes excellence in teaching at their biennial conference. Gallaudet University and the National Black Deaf Association (NBDA) established the Andrew Foster Endowment that offers scholarships to college-bound African-American students. There is the Andrew Foster Auditorium at Gallaudet University, with a bronze bust of Foster installed in front of the auditorium in 2004, a gift from the NBDA.

The most lasting tributes to Foster's legacy are the schools and their students. Today there are over 300 schools in Africa. Where there once was no education for Deaf people, these schools offer elementary and in some cases high school education to their students. Some have managed to send students to Gallaudet University.

Homework 1:5

 CONVERSATION 1

Michelle (A) and Ben (B) demonstrate this dialogue where they introduce themselves. (Note Michelle uses the name "Ann" and Ben uses the name "Sam").

Signer A: Greet, give name, and then ask for name

Signer B: Give name

 A & B: Express pleasure in meeting each other

Key Grammar

WH-WORD QUESTIONS

When you ask questions using spoken English, you use vocal intonation to indicate what kind of question you are asking. For example, asking this English question "Are you a student?" your voice will go up at the end, and if you ask this question "What is your name?", your voice goes down at the end. Similarly, ASL speakers ask questions using facial expressions, head movements, and pauses called non-manual markers. Like English, there are two basic question types in ASL—a wh-word question and a yes-no question. We will discuss the second type in Unit 2 so we will focus on the first type here: a wh-word question. Wh-word questions ask what, who, where, why, how, etc.

To ask a wh-word question, use these non-manual markers:
• furrow brows together
• lean head forward slightly without breaking eye contact with the listener
• hold the last sign (which should be a wh-word sign) until your listener starts to answer

ask for name

🔘 **Ask for Name.** Shown in slow motion, Michelle demonstrates "ask for name" from Conversation 1. Pay close attention to the non-manual markers indicated by the arrows on video.

BEGINNING AND ENDING CONVERSATIONS

Since starting and stopping conversations can sometimes be awkward, especially for people new to ASL, it helps to know how these signs are used:

These two signs are greeting, or salutations.

This sign is used to get attention.

Although the phrase below may be used after an exchange of names, it is also a possible way to wrap up a first meeting.

MAINTAINING EYE CONTACT

Be sure to look at the signer's face, even though you may feel you would understand better if you could focus on their hands. Remember that critical grammar is conveyed with facial expressions, and if you look away, you could miss the whole message. Eventually it will become second nature to focus on the other signer's face when using ASL.

MINIDIALOGUES

David engages in conversations with different people where he asks wh-word questions. Observe the exchange and write what David asked in each minidialogue.

Minidialogue 1: _____

Minidialogue 2: _____

Minidialogue 3: _____

Minidialogue 4: _____

Minidialogue 5: _____

Minidialogue 6: _____

Answers on page 398.

Practice

Practice creating wh-word questions using the three wh-word signs below. Don't forget to furrow your brows, lean your head forward and hold the last sign.

ask what

ask who

ask where

Vocabulary Review   Vocabulary covered in this lesson is on pages 37–38.

Chart of Manual Alphabet

For your reference, here are the handshapes used for the 26 letters of the alphabet.

U   V   W

X   Y   Z

Assignment   List your classmates' names below. Use this chart to help you practice fingerspelling their names.

_____   _____

_____   _____

_____   _____

_____   _____

_____   _____

_____   _____

_____   _____

_____   _____

_____   _____

Homework 1:6

CARDINAL NUMBERS 11–15

Cardinal Numbers 11, 12

As you watch Iva demonstrate these numbers, keep in mind the following:
- palm faces in
- finger(s) "flick" out from underneath thumb twice
- for number 12, keep extended fingers separated

| 11 | 12 |

Cardinal Numbers 13–15

As you watch Iva demonstrate these numbers, notice the following:
- palm faces in
- keep extended fingers closed
- for number 14, tuck thumb in
- move extended fingers toward you twice

| 13 | 14 | 15 |

⊙ Sign the Numbers

Now count up to 15. Try to sign the numbers before Joey, then check if you signed it correctly!

⊙ Circle the Number

In this activity, Joey will sign the numbers. Practice recognizing and distinguishing between numbers that appear similar to each other.

Circle the number signed:

1.	1	2	11	12
2.	2	3	12	13
3.	4	5	14	15
4.	1	2	11	12
5.	2	3	12	13
6.	4	5	14	15
7.	1	2	11	12
8.	2	3	12	13
9.	4	5	14	15
10.	1	2	11	12
11.	2	3	12	13
12.	4	5	14	15

Answers on page 398.

⊙ Write the Number

Now you will see phrases with numbers from 1 to 15. Write down only the number given.

1. _____	6. _____	11. _____
2. _____	7. _____	12. _____
3. _____	8. _____	13. _____
4. _____	9. _____	14. _____
5. _____	10. _____	15. _____

Answers are given in class.

Homework 1:7

 **CULTURAL**

WAYS OF COMMUNICATING WITH OTHERS

As you learn sign, you might bump into Deaf person at work, school, or on the street. Let them know that you sign. If the setting is appropriate and the Deaf person has time, they will be happy to chat with you. If they are in a hurry, the person might excuse himself or herself. In any case, it is important to let the Deaf person be in the lead in setting the communication mode.

Here are strategies Deaf people might use to communicate with you.

Signing. Deaf people are very encouraging of new signers and will be patient with your signing skills. If the conversation is stalling, the Deaf person may switch to another strategy to help along the communication.

Gestures. If signing in ASL doesn't work, the Deaf person may use easily understood gestures to get their message across, pointing, or acting things out.

Writing or typing. This strategy is a sure and clear way to convey a message. When communicating with someone they know, a Deaf person can use email or instant messaging. For "face-to-face' communication messages can be typed out on a pager and shown to the hearing person, or if needed, notes can be written back and forth on a piece of paper.

Third person. In casual settings, a Deaf person may ask a hearing person who signs to relay information for them.

Lipreading and speech. A very small percentage of Deaf people use this strategy, and use it for predictable, limited exchanges of information. For most Deaf people, however, this strategy is not preferred, since it often leads easily to misunderstandings.

Regardless of the strategy, the goal is to communicate. These are the things that you need to remember to do to as new signers:
• Let the Deaf person know you sign
• Avoid spoken English or using voice without relaying information in ASL
• Let the Deaf person set the communication mode

FIST LETTER NAMES

Circle the Name then Cross Out the Name

Tyrone fingerspells one name from each row. For the **first round**, circle the name spelled. For the **second round**, cross out the name spelled.

SUGGESTION: Look over the names below before watching.

1.	Tami	Tim	Tom
2.	Nina	Tina	Ina
3.	Tami	Sina	Sami
4.	Mae	Moe	Mona
5.	Naomi	Toni	Stan
6.	Sean	Sina	Sam
7.	Mimi	Tami	Mia
8.	Ines	Ina	Ian

Answers on page 399.

Write the Name

Write down the name Tyrone gives.

1. _____   4. _____

2. _____   5. _____

3. _____   6. _____

Answers are given in class.

Now, practice fingerspelling the names above until you are comfortable.

DID YOU REALIZE?

The hands on the statue of Abraham Lincoln at the Lincoln Memorial in Washington DC appear to spell out the initials A and L. Legend has it that Daniel Chester French, the famed sculptor, was influenced by his earlier bronze sculpture found on the Gallaudet University campus of Thomas Hopkins Gallaudet teaching a Deaf girl whose hand is forming the letter of her first name, Alice.

CONVERSATION 2

Iva (A) and David (B) demonstrate this conversation where someone else in their immediate environment is identified.

Signer A:	**Spell a name, ask whose name it is**
Signer B:	**Identify who (raise brows)** • **gender** • **brief description** • **point out and glance**
A:	**Glance and nod**
B:	**Affirm (nod)**

Key Grammar

IDENTIFY A PERSON

In class you practiced identifying fellow classmates. Here are some important points to remember.

• **gender**

as you state the person's gender, raise your brows and keep them raised while you finish identifying the person.

• **brief description**

in the description, mention things that will easily distinguish the person from others surrounding him/her. In your description, mention items easily visible such as hair color, shirt color, facial features, eyeglasses, or headwear.

• **point out the person and glance at the person at the same time**

after giving the description, point out the person and glance at him/her. Point with your index finger and with the arm slightly bent.

• **affirm**

after listener confirms s/he knows who you are referring to, you can nod to affirm "that's him/her."

Failure to nod may result in the signer repeating his/her description because s/he assumes you don't know who s/he is referring to.

🔘 *Identify a Person*

Shown in slow motion, David demonstrates how to identify a person from Conversation 2. You will see arrows showing the four points used to identify a person.

tell who: identify person

It's not rude to point in a signing environment. In fact, pointing is used frequently as a sign—to indicate you, others, or an object or location. Pointing is an essential part of ASL. So the next time you spot someone pointing at you, don't worry. They're probably saying something flattering.

🔘 MINIDIALOGUES

View the six video conversations. Answer questions about each conversation. Circle M or F for gender. Write the name spelled. Select the letter of the item and the number of the color and fill in the blanks.

ITEMS

COLORS

1

2

3

4

5

6

7

8

9

10

11

Minidialogue 1

gender: M   F   name: _____

description: color _____ item _____

Minidialogue 2

gender: M   F   name: _____

description: color _____ item _____

Minidialogue 3*

gender: M   F   name: _____

description: color _____ item _____

Minidialogue 4

gender: M   F   name: _____

description: color _____ item _____

Minidialogue 5

gender: M   F   name: _____

description: color _____ item _____

Minidialogue 6

gender: M   F   name: _____

description: color _____ item _____

Answers given in class.

Vocabulary Review   Vocabulary covered in this lesson is on pages 38–40.

* Ben uses a form of the sign for "yellow" that is different from the form you may have learned in class. This modified form indicates a person with "blond hair."

Homework 1:9

INSIDE, ABOVE, AND BELOW

To describe the placement of a shape, name, number, or letter inside, above, or below a shape, follow this sequence:

• trace the shape with both index fingers.

• use your index finger to indicate where to place or locate the secondary item.

• your head, eye gaze, and index fingers should work together to indicate where the second and third items are to be placed.

 ### *Inside, Above, and Below*

David describes the drawings below. Observe how he uses his head, face, eyes, and hands to describe the placement of the number 7.

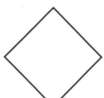

Notice how David:

• looks at the diamond shape as he traces it

• holds the reference point of the diamond with his non-dominant hand

• raises his head and glance above the diamond

• with raised brows, taps to indicate where to place the "7"

Notice how David:

• glances and leans head towards the inside of the diamond

• with raised brows, taps, then signs "7" inside the diamond

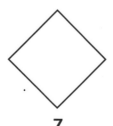

Notice how David:

• lowers his head down and glances below the diamond

• with raised brows, taps, then signs "7" below the diamond

Notice how David:
• uses the same technique for locating the circle and the "7" inside the diamond

Practice
Practice describing the placement of the number "7" in each of the shapes above.

See and Draw
Draw in the boxes what David and Michelle describe on the video. Do not stop the video until David or Michelle completes each description and draw from memory. View the descriptions again to fill in what you missed.

1.	2.	3.
4.	5.	6.
7.	8.	9.

Answers are given in class.

Assignment Practice the descriptions in boxes 1, 3, and 6. Be prepared to show them in class.

Homework 1:10

COMMANDS INVOLVING THE BODY

When giving simple commands to a person for actions involving the body, make your signs firmer and slightly bigger.

🔘 *Commands 1–3*

Watch Joey give the three commands below. Observe him making the signs firmly.

1.

2.

3.

COMMANDS INVOLVING OBJECTS

When giving commands for actions involving objects, not only do you make your signs firmer and slightly bigger, you should raise your brows when naming the object.

🔘 *Commands 4–6*

Watch Joey give three commands involving objects.
Observe him raising his brows when naming the object in the beginning of the command.

4.

5.

6.

Vocabulary Review   Vocabulary covered in this lesson is on pages 41–42.

SIGNING NATURALLY

Homework 1:11

◎ TEST YOUR EYE-Q

David, Ben or Michelle sign two signs or phrases that may be the same or different. Circle either "S" for same or "D" for different. If different, indicate what part of the signs or phrases is different by circling "shape," "name," "sign," or "number."

	Same	Different	If different, tell what is different.			
1.	S	D	shape	name	sign	number
2.	S	D	shape	name	sign	number
3.	S	D	shape	name	sign	number
4.	S	D	shape	name	sign	number
5.	S	D	shape	name	sign	number
6.	S	D	shape	name	sign	number
7.	S	D	shape	name	sign	number
8.	S	D	shape	name	sign	number
9.	S	D	shape	name	sign	number
10.	S	D	shape	name	sign	number
11.	S	D	shape	name	sign	number
12.	S	D	shape	name	sign	number
13.	S	D	shape	name	sign	number
14.	S	D	shape	name	sign	number
15.	S	D	shape	name	sign	number
16.	S	D	shape	name	sign	number
17.	S	D	shape	name	sign	number
18.	S	D	shape	name	sign	number

Answers on page 400.

⊙ PICTURE IT

Do as instructed by Joey, Cinnie, or Tyrone.

1.	**2.**	**3.**
4.	**5.**	**6.**
7.	**8.**	**9.**
10.	**11.**	**12.**

Answers are given in class.

Homework 1:12

CULTURAL

GETTING OTHERS' ATTENTION

There are several ways a Deaf person gets the attention of others.

- **Waving** with one hand is one way to get the attention of other signers. The size of the wave corresponds to the distance between the waver and the other person. A person across the room merits an overhead wave; people sitting across a small table get a slight wave that falls into their field of vision. Showy, theatrical waves might capture the attention of the entire room instead of the person whose attention you want. Opting for a natural and casual hand wave is usually a safe bet.

View. See how Iva waves and how far her hand goes toward Ben.

- **Tapping** is an effective option to get the attention of a person close by if that person faces away from you, or is involved in an activity such as writing, reading, or watching TV. Tap their shoulder or upper arm gently but firmly two or three times. One tap isn't sufficient, and too many taps can convey a sense of urgency or an attitude that you don't intend.

View. See where and how Michelle touches David.

- **Using an intermediary** is done when a signer is not close enough to the intended person to get his or her attention. In these situations, the signer asks the help of an intermediary. The intermediary will either tap or wave to get the person's attention, and direct them to look at the signer.

View. Joey uses Cinnie as an intermediary to get Tyrone's attention.

QUESTIONS TO ASK

Now that you have reached the end of Unit 1, you should be able to ask the following questions. Read the cue for each question below, think about how you would sign it, and watch Cinnie sign the question on the video.

1. ask the person's name

2. (point out two students), ask if they have the same name

3. (spell a name), ask who it is

4. (name an object), ask where it is

5. (perform an action), ask what you did

6. (describe two things), ask if they are the same

7. (name members of a category), ask what the category is

8. (point to an object), ask what it is

9. (point to an item or name an object), ask what color it is

◉ MINIDIALOGUES

Watch these minidialogues and write your answer in the blanks.

Minidialogue 1

What does Tom look like? _____

_____

Does the woman remember all the men and women's names?

_____

What are the two women's (the signer and the woman in the

orange jacket) names? _____

_____

Minidialogue 2

What color does David think Michelle's shoes are? _____

The woman's shoes are the same color as whose shoes?

_____

What is that person's name? _____

What color are David's shoes? _____

Minidialogue 3

What color paper does Joey ask Tyrone to take? _____

What does Joey ask Tyrone to draw? _____

Where does Joey tell Tyrone to write his name? _____

_____

What does Joey correct in Tyrone's drawing? _____

_____

Answers on page 401.

SELF-ASSESSMENT

Now that you are done with this unit, rate yourself using the list below: 5 being the most comfortable and confident you feel about your skill in the area and 1 being the least.

NOTE: If you marked 3 or below on any skill area, you should review that portion of the workbook.

1.	I know how to introduce myself (fingerspell my name, ask for a name, and express pleasure in meeting someone).	5	4	3	2	1
2.	I know how to identify a person (gender + brief description).	5	4	3	2	1
3.	I know appropriate ways to get a person's attention.	5	4	3	2	1
4.	I can follow classroom instructions.	5	4	3	2	1
5.	I know how to describe a shape and how to indicate where to place secondary items.	5	4	3	2	1
6.	I know how to correctly use facial expressions and head position to ask wh-word questions.	5	4	3	2	1
7.	I know the correct hand positions for fingerspelling.	5	4	3	2	1
8.	I know the correct handshapes for fist letters.	5	4	3	2	1
9.	I can read and sign the numbers 1–15.	5	4	3	2	1
10.	I can discriminate between descriptions – telling specifically what is the same and what is different.	5	4	3	2	1
11.	I know how to give commands involving objects and the body.	5	4	3	2	1
12.	I know the vocabulary covered in this unit.	5	4	3	2	1

Greetings

 or

Name

be named; name

Wh-Word Question Signs

used to ask what, as in a definition

used to ask who, as in identification of a person

used to ask for the location of something

Response

express pleasure in meeting someone

Gender

an individual, a person

Clothing

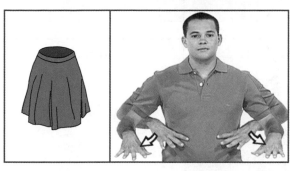

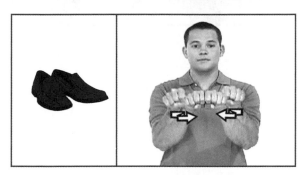

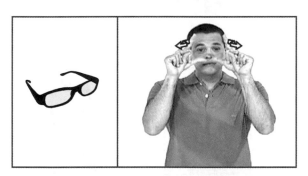

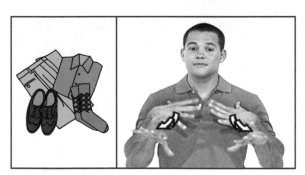

Appearance

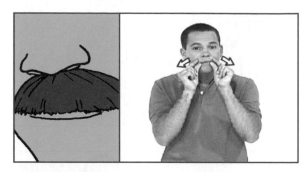

Colors

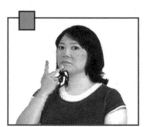

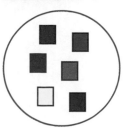

Commands involving the body

Commands involving objects

OBJECTS

ACTIONS

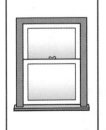

OBJECTS

ACTIONS

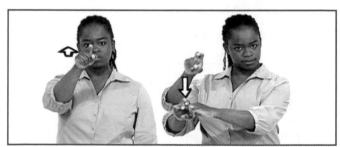

Same – Different

Categories

 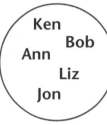

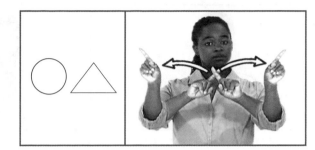 

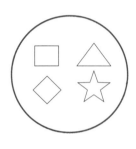 

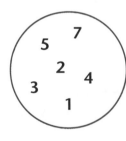 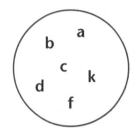

Memory

to recall, to remember   unable to recall, to forget

to ask to repeat; do again

to be correct

to be incorrect

to imitate; make same;
to copy

to fingerspell

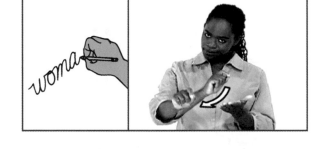

to write down something short or
quickly, to jot down

assignment to do at home

Field of Poppies
Granville Redmond

"This painting reveals Redmond's love for
the more intimate rural views of California's
topography...a field of yellow poppies, or a
landscape with a glimpse of the sea beyond.
Redmond may be seen as a transitional
figure among California landscape painters
of the early 20th century."

-Deborah Meranski Sonnenstrahl,
Deaf Artists in America

UNIT 2

Exchanging Personal Information

Homework 2:1

⊙ CONVERSATION 1

Cinnie (A) and Tyrone (B) demonstrate this dialogue where they discuss personal information other than their names. Here they ask yes–no questions and give *affirmative* responses.

Signer A:	**Ask if student**
Signer B:	**Affirm**
A:	**Ask if hearing**
B:	**Affirm**
A:	**Ask if learning ASL**
B:	**Affirm**
A:	**Ask if learning at (name of school)**
B:	**Affirm**
A:	**Respond**

⊙ CONVERSATION 2

Ben (A) and Tyrone (B) demonstrate this dialogue where *negative* responses are given to yes-no questions.

Signer A:	**Ask if deaf**
Signer B:	**Negate, correct information**
A:	**Ask if teacher**
B:	**Negate, correct information**
A:	**Ask if learning (name another language)**
B:	**Negate, correct information**
A:	**Ask if learning at (name another college)**
B:	**Negate, correct information**
A:	**Respond**

YES–NO QUESTIONS

A yes-no question requires a "yes" or "no" answer. Examples of yes-no questions are "Do you have any children?," "Do you like coffee?," or "Are you a student?"

To ask a yes–no question in ASL, use these non-manual markers:
• raise brows throughout the question
• lean head forward with the last sign
• hold the last sign until your listener starts to answer.

💿 *Yes–No Questions*

Cinnie demonstrates "ask if hearing" from Conversation 1. Pay close attention to the non-manual markers indicated by the arrows.

ask if hearing

Responses to Yes–No Questions

It's important that you nod when affirming information and shake your head when negating information. Additionally, after a negative response, you should give the correct information. To answer without non-manual markers is like speaking in a monotone voice—boring!

See Tyrone and Ben demonstrate affirmative and negative
responses to Cinnie's question above.

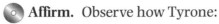 **Affirm.** Observe how Tyrone:
- begins nodding just before responding
- continues nodding until the end of the sentence .

affirm you are hearing

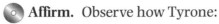 **Negate and Correct.** Observe how Ben:
- begins shaking his head just before responding
- nods when giving the correct information.

negate, then tell you are deaf

Sign Tip

Fluent ASL communication flows smoothly, and active listening—
also called feedback—is expected. Respond to the signer with
gentle nods, brief signs, and facial expressions that show your
understanding and interest in what is being said.

The listener has an active role in the rhythm of the conversation.
In the absence of feedback, signers may assume you do not understand and may repeat information. Make your active listening
visual by acknowledging information as you process it.

Acknowledge Information

One way to make your listening active is to use this sign with nodding:

acknowledge information

Examples of this sign are found in Conversations 1 & 2 when Cinnie and Ben acknowledge the information that Tyrone gives.

A SIGN OF CAUTION: the signs at right are not used as active listening. These signs have different meanings and functions.

this sign is used to answer a question affirmatively

this sign is used to confirm something, or to state something is correct

MAKING CONNECTIONS

One of the things you need to know when making connections with Deaf people is what to expect when you meet someone, and what to expect when getting to know someone. Connections in the Deaf world are important, and upon meeting information exchanged will help determine your connection to the Deaf community.

Here are some things commonly shared upon meeting.

First and Last Names
You need to be able to spell your first and last name. The Deaf person will also spell their first and last name. Don't be shy to ask them to spell their name several times until you understand it.

Deaf or Hearing
Deaf people, even from different countries all over the world, have many shared experiences. Finding out if a person is Deaf or hearing is a way to move the introduction in an appropriate direction. The Deaf person will ask different questions about a person's background and experience in the Deaf community depending on the answer.

If You Are Hearing
After exchanging names, and establishing that you are hearing, a Deaf person may ask where you are learning ASL, whether or not your teacher is Deaf, the first and last name of your teacher, and possibly why you are learning ASL. This begins your "connection."

If You Are Deaf
After exchanging names, and establishing you are Deaf, a Deaf person will ask where you grew up, if you went to a Deaf school, what years you went to school there, whether or not you went to Gallaudet--and if yes—which class (i.e., the Class of 1975). Based on these questions, the conversation might move to discussing people you might know in common.

Deepening the Connection
Within the Deaf community, Deaf people strengthen social bonds by participating in various community activities like sports, clubs,conferences, and other social events. Former classmates, co-workers, friends and acquaintances travel for miles to attend these Deaf events, maintaining contact with each other and sharing news about themselves, mutual friends,and the community at large—expanding their connection to the community.

To start your connection to the Deaf community, you need to able to introduce yourself, and give information about your class and teacher (so learn how to spell your teacher's first and last name). Remember the first and last name of the Deaf person you meet, so you can tell your teacher about meeting them. Your teacher may know the Deaf person you meet, and sharing that information with your teacher shows that you are fostering your own connections.

MINIDIALOGUES

Watch the two video minidialogues and answer the questions below. Observe the signers respond by either affirming, or negating and correcting information.

Minidialogue 1

1. Do Norman and Priscilla attend the same college?

2. What language(s) are they learning? Who are their teacher(s)?

Minidialogue 2

1. Who are Stefanie and Iva talking about?

2. What do the people they are discussing have in common?

3. In what ways are they different?

Answers are given in class.

Vocabulary Review Vocabulary Review for this lesson is on pages 92–94.

WHICH HAND DO I USE?

All signers have a dominant and a non-dominant hand. If you are right-handed, your right hand is dominant; if left-handed, your left hand is dominant. If you are ambidextrous, choose one hand as your dominant hand and be consistent with its use.

All of the signers on your DVD are right-handed. If you are left-handed, you can mirror the movements of the signers. Right-handed students will need to copy from the perspective of the signer. If you are unsure, stand next to your TV monitor so that you and the signer on the DVD are facing in the same direction, then check to see if you are signing correctly.

One-handed signs. Always use your dominant hand for words signed with one hand. For example:

Two-handed symmetrical signs. Both your dominant and non-dominant hands are used for two-handed signs in symmetrical movements. For example:

 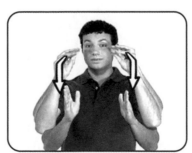 

Two-handed non-symmetrical signs. The dominant hand moves while the non-dominant hand remains stationary for these signs. For example:

 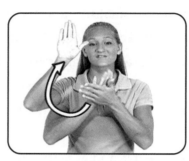 

Carefully observe how your ASL teacher forms each sign as she or he introduces it. Be sure you are consistent in the use of your dominant and non-dominant hands.

Now review the signs you have learned so far and identify which of the three categories they belong to—one-handed, two-handed symmetrical, or two-handed non-symmetrical. Be ready to share your list in class.

Gallaudet

GALLAUDET UNIVERSITY

Gallaudet University, located in Washington DC, holds a special place in the Deaf World. Since President Abraham Lincoln signed an act to establish the school in 1864, the school remains a celebrated and internationally influential institution. It is the only Deaf liberal arts university in the world and is both a repository of American Sign Language, Deaf culture and history, and an inspiring setting for higher learning.

Deaf people and other people interested in the Deaf World, from all over the United States and worldwide, look to Gallaudet as a leader in education and research. The Gallaudet Research Institute is the source of demographic and educational data regarding Deaf people in the U.S., and continually innovates in the field of Deaf education. The university offers over 80 undergraduate and graduate degrees in more than 20 disciplines. The Laurent Clerc National Deaf Education Center's two demonstration schools, and six regional centers serve Deaf students throughout the United States.

Over the years, thousands of Gallaudet graduates successfully contributed and still contribute to professional fields as educators, writers, lawyers, actors, entrepreneurs, researchers, CEOs, CFOs, artists, therapists, social workers, and in many other professional roles. Gallaudet Alumni also bring the spirit, pride, and accomplishments of their Gallaudet experience back home, often becoming leaders in their own communities.

As a place of cultural significance and a recognized center of a Deaf-World social network that spans the national and international arenas, Gallaudet has been called a beacon, Deaf Mecca, and "home" by its graduates, visiting scholars and supporters.

As a place of cultural significance and a recognized center of a Deaf-World social network that spans the national and international arenas, Gallaudet has been called a beacon, Deaf Mecca, and "home" by its graduates, visiting scholars and supporters. The Gallaudet Archives contains the world's largest collection of materials documenting the language and culture of Deaf people. Gallaudet University also hosted Deaf Way I in 1989, with over 5,000 people from 80 countries gathering to share ideas, talents, art and visual performance, and information about Deaf life. In 2002, Deaf Way II drew over 10,000 people from 120 countries, creating a Deaf global village filled with arts, entertainment and cultural exchange.

While Gallaudet's role on a large scale is unquestioned, the college experience it offers to each class leaves lasting and dear memories in the hearts and minds of students. The school's mascot is the Bison, its school paper the Buff and Blue. Friendships formed are lasting, with Alumni Associations throughout the United States and Lifetime Members of the Alumni Association numbering in the thousands.

Trivia Question...

Who signs the diploma when students graduate from Gallaudet?

a) the President of the University

b) the Majority leader of the House

c) the President of the United States

d) the President of the National Association of the Deaf

Answer given in class.

💿 CARDINAL NUMBERS 16–19

As you watch Iva demonstrate these numbers, keep in mind the following:

• begin with the "A" handshape, palm facing you

• twist your hand so the palm faces out to make the second number 6, 7, 8, or 9. (Remember the thumb does not overlap the finger used to make the second number)

  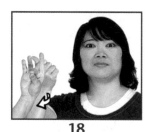 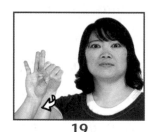

| 16 | 17 | 18 | 19 |

💿 *Sign the Numbers*

Now you count from 16 to 19. Try to sign the number before Joey, then check to see if you've signed it correctly!

💿 *Circle the Number*

In this activity Joey will sign the number. Practice recognizing and distinguishing between numbers that appear similar to each other.

Circle the number signed:

1.	16	17	18	19
2.	16	17	18	19
3.	16	17	18	19
4.	16	17	18	19
5.	6	16	9	19
6.	6	16	9	19
7.	6	16	9	19
8.	6	16	9	19

9.	7	17	8	18
10.	7	17	8	18
11.	7	17	8	18
12.	7	17	8	18

Answers on page 402.

Write the Number

Now practice understanding numbers. You will see numbers from 1–19. Write down the number signed.

1. _____	7. _____	13. _____
2. _____	8. _____	14. _____
3. _____	9. _____	15. _____
4. _____	10. _____	16. _____
5. _____	11. _____	17. _____
6. _____	12. _____	18. _____

Answers are given in class.

Variations 1 and 2

Signs may vary in different parts of the United States and Canada. On video, Joey demonstrates examples of two variations used for the numbers 16–19.

16 (variation 1)

16 (variation 2)

Homework 2:3

ask if ready (to begin)

TIC-TAC-TOE

Ben and Tyrone play the game Tic-Tac-Toe. Mark the squares indicated by the players with an X or an O. Remember to take the signer's perspective to locate the square. If you have difficulty with this, orient your body so you and the signer are facing the same direction.

When you see Ben or Tyrone use this sign, be ready to mark the grid. Let the games begin!

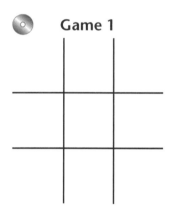

Game 1   Game 2   Game 3

View the games again and observe how Tyrone and Ben use the following sequence to identify where to place an "X" or "O":
• use raised brows to establish reference with non-dominant hand
• hold reference point as dominant hand counts off squares until it reaches the right square
• use raised brows when tapping repeatedly to indicate "here" before signing "X" or "O" in the spot.

Notice also how their eye gaze and use of space correlate with the visualized grid.

Answers on page 402.

Vocabulary Review   Vocabulary Review associated with this game is on page 95.

Homework 2:4

LANGUAGE BACKGROUNDS: TRANSITIONS

When telling about your language background, organize the information chronologically beginning with your native language(s) and then telling about languages learned during different periods in your life. To transition from one time period to the next, raise your brows while mentioning the period (high school, college, etc.).

 Carol's Language Background

Cinnie narrates "Carol's Language Background" using these transitions:

transition 1
name of subject/topic

transition 2
high school time

transition 3
college time

transition 4
present time

Practice signing the narrative, raising your brows to signal each transition.

Vocabulary Review   Vocabulary Review for this activity is on pages 95–97.

⊙ *Language Backgrounds 1 and 2*

Watch the two narratives and fill in the blanks below.

Language Background 1

1. name: _____

   languages she grew up with: _____

2. **high school time**

   -other language(s) learned:_____

   -number of years:_____

   -how much language remembered:

   |————|————|————|————|
   100%   0%

3) **college time**

   -other language(s) learned:_____

   -number of years:_____

   -how much language remembered:

   |————|————|————|————|
   100%   0%

4) **present time**

   -other language(s) currently learning:_____

   -level of difficulty:

   |————|————|————|
   very difficult   *very easy*

Language Background 2

---

1. name: _____

    languages he grew up with: _____

2. high school time

    -other language(s) learned:_____

    -number of years:_____

    -how much language remembered:

    |———+———+———+———|
    100%   0%

3) college time

    -other language(s) learned:_____

    -number of years:_____

    -how much language remembered:

    |———+———+———+———|
    100%   0%

4) present time
    -other language(s) currently learning:_____

    -level of difficulty:

    |———+———+———+———|
  very difficult   *very easy*

Answers are given in class.

View both narratives again and practice signing along. Be sure to raise your brows to signal a transition for each of these listed below:
• name of subject/topic
• high school time
• college time
• present time

Your Language Background

Fill in the blanks with information about your own language experience. Then rehearse the information to sign in class. Remember to raise your brows to signal a transition.

---

1. name: _____

    languages she grew up with: _____

2. high school time

    -other language(s) learned:_____

    -number of years:_____

    -how much language remembered:

```
  |----+----+----+----|
100%              0%
```

3) college time

    -other language(s) learned:_____

    -number of years:_____

    -how much language remembered:

```
  |----+----+----+----|
100%              0%
```

4) present time
    -other language(s) currently learning:_____

    -level of difficulty:

```
  |----+----+----|
very difficult   very easy
```

Homework 2:5

UP LETTERS

Here you practice letters with "up" handshapes, which include the following—**B C D F K L R U V W X.**

All of these letters, except the letters "C" and "X," have finger(s) fully extended upward. The letters "C" and "X" have bent fingers.

 View. Cinnie demonstrates the dos and don'ts of forming "up" letters.

The letter "B"
• fingers extend upward and are closed
• thumb crosses loosely in front of the palm

The letter "C"
• thumb and palm faces forward, not sideways

The letter "D"
• middle finger and thumb make a flat "O" shape
• index finger extends upward
• ring and pinkie fingers softly curl downward toward the palm

The letter "F"
- index finger and thumb make a flat "O" shape
- thumb and index finger do not overlap
- rest of the fingers extend upward and are spread out slightly

The letter "K"
- thumb contacts the middle finger at the knuckle
- middle finger extends forward and slightly upward
- index finger extends straight upward

The letter "L"
- thumb extends to the side and index finger extends upward
- the rest of the fingers sit in a relaxed manner over the heel of the palm

The letter "R"
- middle finger crosses over the index finger

> **NOTE:** The letter that precedes or follows the letter "R" will determine exactly how the thumb is positioned, i.e. the thumb is touching or not touching the ring finger.

The letter "U"
- index and middle fingers extend upward and are closed.
- thumb overlaps the ring finger

The letter "V"
- index and middle fingers extend upward and are spread apart
- thumb overlaps the ring finger

The letter "W"
• three main fingers extend upward and are spread apart
• pinkie finger and thumb do not overlap

The letter "X" (at the beginning of a name or word)
• index finger is bent
• thumb is tucked in, resting on the middle finger
• palm faces out

The letter "X" (in the middle or at the end of a name or word)
• palm faces to the side
• the hand tilts forward

 Sign the Letters
Copy Melinda as she demonstrates how to form these letter combinations.

1.	al	ax			7.	ka	ke	kr	ku
2.	ba	be	br	bu	8.	la	le	li	lo	lu
3.	ca	ck			9.	ol			
4.	da	de	di	dr	10.	ra	ro	rl	rt
5.	el	ed	er		11.	sa	sl	su	
6.	fr				12.	va	wa		

Challenge Yourself   Get a blank sheet of paper and view "Sign the Letters" again. Write the combinations down and compare with the list above.

Practice spelling these letter combinations on your own. Take care to articulate the letters clearly and precisely. Do not "bounce" or "stamp" each letter.

UP LETTER NAMES

Circle the Name

Tyrone fingerspells one name from each question below. Circle the name spelled.

1.	Carl	Earl	9.	Rima	Rita
2.	Dawn	Dean	10.	Bea	Bert
3.	Dana	Dan	11.	Ben	Ken
4.	Cara	Cole	12.	Mike	Mel
5.	Kurt	Burt	13.	Lilli	Lon
6.	Fran	Fred	14.	Ed	Di
7.	Dale	Kali	15.	Van	Val
8.	Ted	Ned	16.	Max	Alex

Answers on page 403.

Number the Names

For each question, order the names that Tyrone fingerspells 1, 2, or 3. When done, practice fingerspelling all the names. Remember to make letters flow—no "bouncing" or "stamping."

1. _____Olin   3. _____Cara
   _____Eli   _____Kris
   _____Carol   _____Karl

2. _____Carl   4. _____Cole
   _____Edna   _____Burt
   _____Rick   _____Rima

Answers on page 403.

Homework 2:6

WHO ENJOYS WHAT?

Michelle identifies a person and tells what activity that person enjoys doing. Draw a line from the picture of the person to the picture of the activity that matches the information given.

PERSON

ACTIVITY

Answers are given in class.

Vocabulary Review   Vocabulary Review for this lesson is on pages 98–100.

REGINA OLSON HUGHES (1895-1993)

Regina Olson Hughes, the most renowned Deaf scientific illustrator, took her love of flowers and art and turned it into a lasting contribution to science.

Hughes was born in 1895 in Herman, Nebraska. As a child she loved drawing and flowers, one time remarking, "We used to get five cents for ice cream cones. I would never buy ice cream, I would buy flower seeds." She became Deaf at the age of 14. She became skilled at sign language when she enrolled at Gallaudet University (then College). Hughes earned her Bachelor's degree in 1918 and her Master's in 1920.

She married Dr. Frederick Hughes in 1923 (the Hughes Gymnasium, demolished in 1999 was named in honor of his distinguished 40-year career at the school) and lived on the Gallaudet campus for thirty years.

In a time when women hardly entered the workforce, Hughes got a job for the State Department as a language translator, since her fascination with languages had inspired her to learn German, French, Spanish, Portuguese, Italian and some Latin. By 1925, Hughes was hired by the Department of Agriculture, quickly becoming an illustrator after her artistic talents were recognized. Almost completely self-educated in botany, her illustrations appeared in numerous publications, including textbooks. Her personal oil paitings were shown at the International Exhibition of Fine and Applied Arts by Deaf Artists in 1934.

She is the only Deaf artist to have a solo exhibition at the Smithsonian Institution. A plant species Hughesia reginae, and a type of daisy, Billbergia reginae were named in her honor.

She received many honors as a result of her excellent work, receiving the Superior Service Award for her original scientific drawings. Her paintings and illustrations were exhibited in solo and group shows, and her orchid painting are permanently on view at the Museum of Natural History, Smithsonian Institution. Hughes received an honorary doctorate from Gallaudet University in 1967.

Hughes exhibited through the Washington Water Color Association for twenty years and the Guild of Natural Science Illustrators for eighteen years. She is the only Deaf artist to have a solo exhibition at the Smithsonian Institutiion. A plant species *Hughesia reginae*, and a type of daisy, *Billbergia reginae* were named in her honor. Hughes continued to sketch and paint into her nineties. She died in August 1993.

The Estate of Regina Olson Hughes donated a collection of letters, photos, and illustrations to The Gallaudet University Archives in 1993. Her outstanding work was matched by an unassuming demeanor, but Hughes's zest for life and beauty lives on in her sketches and paintings.

Homework 2:7

◎ CARDINAL NUMBERS 20–29

As you watch Iva demonstrate these numbers, keep in mind the following:

• for all numbers, begin with the "L" handshape except for the number "22," which uses the "V" handshape

• the palm faces out except for the number "22," which has the palm facing down

• for numbers "20" and "21," the movement is repeated twice and the hand stays in place

• number "22" has a stamping movement, with the hand moving to the side to form the second stamp

• numbers 23–29 start with an handshape "L" in an upright position. Move your hand slightly forward when signing the second number.

20	21	22	23
24	25	26	
27	28	29	

Sign the Numbers

Now count from 20 to 29. Try to sign the number before Joey, then check to see if you've signed it correctly!

Circle the Number

Joey will sign one number for each question. Practice recognizing and distinguishing between numbers that appear similar by circling the numbers signed.

Circle the number signed:

1.	23	24	25	26
2.	20	21	22	27
3.	26	27	28	29
4.	23	24	25	26
5.	20	21	22	27
6.	26	27	28	29
7.	23	24	25	26
8.	20	21	22	27
9.	26	27	28	29
10.	23	24	25	26
11.	20	21	22	27
12.	26	27	28	29

Answers on page 404.

Write the Number

For each row, Iva and Joey tell you, in random order, how many there are of each item. Write the number signed under the correct picture.

ROW A

_____   _____   _____   _____

ROW B

ROW C

ROW D

ROW E

ROW F

Practice on Your Own. Increase your fluency, go back and practice signing the number phrases above.

Answers are given in class.

Homework 2:8

 ## DESCRIBING SHAPES

How to describe a shape depends upon the type of shape. There are three types of shapes:
- symmetrical
- asymmetrical
- linear

 ### *Symmetrical*

See how Stefanie moves both hands simultaneously to trace both sides of this shape.

 ### *Asymmetrical*

See how Stefanie holds her non-dominant hand as a reference point and traces this shape with her dominant hand.

Linear

 See how Stefanie holds her non-dominant hand as a reference point, and traces this linear shape.

Signer's Perspective

You must take the *signer's perspective*, or see the shape as if through the signer's eyes, to correctly draw the shapes here, especially asymmetrical or linear shapes.

Stefanie describes one of the lines below. Decide which line represents the description. Check your answer by replaying the segment. If you are still confused, stand next to the TV so that you and the signer are looking in the same direction. Answer is given at the bottom of this page.

> **NOTE:** If a shape is circular, follow the method for asymmetrical or linear shapes, holding the non-dominant hand as a reference point and tracing the circle with the dominant hand.

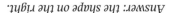

Answer: the shape on the right.

◉ *Draw the Shape*

Stefanie first describes a basic shape, then adds another shape or line inside, above, below, or next to the shape. Find the basic shape Stefanie describes, then draw the second shape in the appropriate spot. Remember to take the signer's perspective to decide where to place the second shape.

Answers are given in class.

Homework 2:9

 CONVERSATION 3

Stefanie (A) and Priscilla (B) demonstrate this dialogue where
another person is identified by his gender, action, and appearance.

Signer A:	Identify person (gender + action)
Signer B:	Add description to confirm (appearance)
A:	Confirm
B:	Respond (nod to confirm)
A:	Ask question about the person
B:	Respond
A:	Suggest activity all three can do together
B:	Agree

Key Grammar

opener

IDENTIFY PEOPLE WHO ARE PRESENT

When identifying someone visible to you and your listener, follow
this sequence.

• **use this opener**

   This sign is used to direct the listener's attention to the location
   of the person to whom the signer is referring. So, if the person
   being referred to is on your right, the sign would move to the
   right. If the person is on your left, the sign would move to the left.

• **describe the person**

   Give the person's gender and one or more of the following:
   appearance, body position, or action.

• **glance toward and point to the person to whom you are referring**

• **raise your brows**

   Keep your brows raised throughout your description until your
   listener confirms that she or he knows to whom you are referring.

• **listener confirms**

Your listener should glance at the person to whom you are referring and confirm that they understand by nodding. Sometimes the listener may need to add to the description of the person to whom you are referring in order to confirm. In that situation, you may need to either affirm or correct their additional information.

Identify People

See how Stefanie identifies a person and Pricilla glances and confirms the person being referred to by adding to the description.

identify person

MINIDIALOGUES

View the three minidialogues. Give information about each conversation by circling M or F for gender, selecting how the person was identified and writing down what information was given about the person.

Minidialogue 1

gender: M   F

how was the person identified (check all that apply):

❑ appearance   ❑ body position   ❑ action

information given about person:

_____

_____

_____

Minidialogue 2

gender: M   F

how was the person identified (check all that apply):

❏ appearance   ❏ body position   ❏ action

information given about person:

_____

_____

_____

Minidialogue 3

gender: M   F

how was the person identified (check all that apply):

❏ appearance   ❏ body position   ❏ action

information given about person:

_____

_____

_____

Answers are given in class.

Vocabulary Review   Vocabulary Review for this lesson is on pages 100–105.

⊙ NAMES AND TIDBITS

Norman identifies six people from below and gives some information about each one. Write the information in the appropriate blanks below.

Answers are given in class.

Homework 2:10

 DOUBLE LETTER NAMES

Cinnie demonstrates how to fingerspell names with double letters in these three categories:

• **Bobby.** When spelling names with "bb," "kk," "ll," and "rr," the double letter is repeated twice with a bounce. Observe Cinnie fingerspell the name "Bobby."

• **Bessie.** When spelling names with "ss," "nn," "tt," "ff," "dd," and "mm," the double letter is repeated twice without a bounce. Observe Cinnie fingerspell the name "Bessie."

• **Aaron.** When spelling names with "aa," "ee," and "oo," the double letter moves sideways and is usually not repeated. Observe Cinnie fingerspell the name "Aaron."

 View. Melinda demonstrates how to fingerspell these names with double letters.

Letters that Bounce

Carrie

Nikki

Willie

Letters without a Bounce

Danny

Duffy

Kitty

Maddy

Timmy

Letters that Move Sideways

Lee

Yoon

Circle the Name

Circle the name Tyrone spells.

1.	Libby	Lilly	Linny	
2.	Dolly	Danny	Donny	Debby
3.	Etta	Emma	Ella	
4.	Emmie	Eddie	Ellie	Effie
5.	Manny	Matty	Maddy	

Answers on page 404.

Fill in the Blank

Fill in the blank with the correct letters from the names Tyrone fingerspells.

1.	Lo____ie	11.	Pa____y
2.	Lo____ie	12.	Pa____y
3.	Do____ie	13.	____n
4.	Do____ie	14.	____n
5.	Ki____y	15.	W____y
6.	Ki____y	16.	W____y
7.	Ta____y	17.	Te____y
8.	Ta____y	18.	Te____y
9.	Ke____y		
10.	Ke____y		

Answers on page 405.

Write the Name

Write the name Tyrone fingerspells.

1. _____	5. _____
2. _____	6. _____
3. _____	7. _____
4. _____	8. _____

Answers are given in class.

Homework 2:11

ask to be pardoned, "excuse me"

NEGOTIATING A SIGNING ENVIRONMENT

Walk Through

Whenever possible, opt to go around, rather than through, a conversation. If there is no choice but to pass through a conversation, pass quickly so the signers won't be interrupted. Don't hunch down or wait to be acknowledged by the signers. This disrupts their exchange, since it is much more visually distracting. While not expected, you may sign "excuse me" as you pass through.

View. Watch how Isias walks through Stefanie and Priscilla's conversation.

Use Touch

When your path is too narrow to pass between several groups of signers, it is customary to press someone's shoulder or upper back, and they will move aside while remaining engaged in their conversation. Avoid tapping, unless you need a person to move more than a few steps aside. Tapping prompts the person to turn toward you, breaking their conversation.

View. Watch how Melinda touches Priscilla to move her aside and see how Priscilla stays engaged in her conversation with Norman.

Ask Person to Move

People can sometimes unknowingly block your view. If it isn't possible to adjust your position so you can see, you should ask people to move by pressing their shoulder in the direction that would clear your view.

View. Priscilla lets Norman know she needs him to sit back by pressing the front of his shoulder so she can see Isias.

Homework 2:12

CONVERSATION STRATEGY: ASKING WHAT IS THE SIGN

As you learn ASL, you might forget some signs or need to use signs other than those taught in class. To ask for a sign you've forgotten or don't know, use the phrase below and the following strategies.

ask what is the sign

Strategies

Norman (A) demonstrates five (5) different strategies to ask for a sign. Priscilla (B) and Stefanie (C) give various responses.

⊙ *Point to Object*

Signer A:	(points to object) Asks for sign
Signer B:	Gives sign
Signer C:	Confirms Signer B's answer

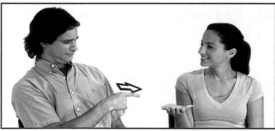

strategy: point to object

respond: give the sign

⊙ *Draw Object*

Signer A:	(draws object) Asks for sign
Signer B:	Tells Signer A she forgot the sign
Signer C:	Gives the sign

strategy: draw object

respond: apologize for forgetting the sign

⊙ *List Items in a Category*

Signer A:	(lists items in a category) Asks for a sign
Signer B:	Tells she doesn't know the sign
Signer C:	Gives the sign

strategy: list items in category

respond: doesn't know the sign

⊙ Use Opposites

> **Signer A:** (uses opposites) Asks for a sign
> **Signer B:** Tells they think you know the sign
> **Signer C:** Confirms Signer B's answer

strategy: use opposites   respond: thinks the sign is....

⊙ Describe/Act Out

> **Signer A:** (describes/acts out) Asks for a sign
> **Signer B:** Asks for clarification
> **Signer C:** Clarifies
> **Signer B:** Gives the sign (incorrectly)
> **Signer C:** Gives the correct sign

strategy: describe/
act out

respond: ask for clarification

Remember ASL and English are different languages, so finger-spelling an English word doesn't guarantee you will get the correct ASL sign. It is best to use these strategies (point, draw, use opposites, list things in a given category, describe, or act out) to get the sign you need.

Memory Game

This is a great way to review vocabulary you've learned so far. You can get together with other students and use these strategies in a game – you ask for a sign and others must recall the sign. Remember to only ask for signs you've learned in class. To keep the game interesting, give a point for every sign recalled correctly. At the end of the game, the one who recalled the most signs is treated to a free drink.

DID YOU REALIZE?

The circular football huddle was invented in 1894 when the Gallaudet University team quarterback Paul Hubbard realized the opposing Deaf teams could understand their signed play calls on the field. Hubbard gathered his players in a close circle to call plays, and the tradition of the football huddle was born.

QUESTIONS TO ASK

Now that you have reached the end of Unit 2, you should be able to ask the following questions. Read the cue for each question below, think about how you would sign it, and watch Ben sign the question on video. Find a partner and practice signing the questions (and answers) to each other.

1. ask if the person is hearing

2. ask if the person was raised speaking both English and French

3. ask if the person learned Spanish in high school

4. ask if the person still remembers his/her Spanish

5. ask if learning ASL is easy

6. ask the person if s/he wants an apple

7. ask if the person likes to travel

8. ask if the person prefers to drink soda pop

9. ask the person what is the sum of 23 + 3

10. ask if the person detests reading

WHICH IS THE BEST RESPONSE?

Check the Box. Norman gives two different responses to Iva's questions. Determine which response is correct and check that box.

	Response 1	Response 2
1.	☐	☐
2.	☐	☐
3.	☐	☐
4.	☐	☐
5.	☐	☐

Answers on page 405.

 **AUTOBIOGRAPHIES**

In each of the three narratives, the signers assume a "role" and share information about themselves. Summarize the information.

Autobiography 1

Name _____

Personal information: Deaf or hearing _____

Language background: _____

What he is doing now: _____

Likes/dislikes: _____

Favorite color: _____

Autobiography 2

Name _____

Personal information: Deaf or hearing _____

Language background: _____

Likes/dislikes: _____

Favorite color: _____

Autobiography 3

Name _____

Personal information: Deaf or hearing _____

Language background: _____

Likes/dislikes: _____

Favorite color: _____

Answers on pages 406.

Your Autobiography

Prepare your presentation:

- fill in the blanks below
- review "Transitions," page 61
- review the three narratives from "Autobiographies," page 89 and identify the transitions
- identify where to place transitions in your own narrative
- practice the information until you no longer need to refer to the paper.

Name _____ Deaf or hearing _____

Language(s) raised using _____

Language(s) taken in: High School _____

number of years _____

how much s/he still remembers _____

College _____

number of years _____

how much s/he still remembers _____

present _____

where _____

level of difficulty |——————|——————|——————|

very difficult   *very easy*

Likes: _____ Dislikes: _____

Favorite leisure activity: _____ Favorite color: _____

Presenting Your Autobiography

- Begin by giving your name.
- Present the information without looking at the paper. Remember to raise your brows and to pause slightly before you begin to talk about the next topic or time frame relating to your language background.

SELF-ASSESSMENT

Now that you are done with this unit, rate yourself using the list below: 5 indicates feeling the most comfortable and confident about your skill in that area and 1 indicates feeling the least confident.

NOTE: If you marked 3 or below on any skill area, you should review that portion of the workbook.

		5	4	3	2	1
1.	I know how to ask a yes/no question.	5	4	3	2	1
2.	I know how to identify a person (gender, appearance, body position, and/or action) and either ask a question or make a statement about the person.	5	4	3	2	1
3.	I know the correct way to acknowledge information signed by the other person.	5	4	3	2	1
4.	I know how to narrate my language background using transitions (raised brows) to signal a new time frame.	5	4	3	2	1
5.	I know how to narrate information about a person and to use transitions (raised brows) to move from one topic to the next.	5	4	3	2	1
6.	I know how to describe three different types of shapes and how to indicate where to place secondary items. I can take the signer's perspective to draw a shape.	5	4	3	2	1
7.	I know appropriate ways to negotiate through a signed conversation and through crowds of people conversing in signs.	5	4	3	2	1
8.	I know the correct hand position for fingerspelling names with double letters.	5	4	3	2	1
9.	I know correct handshapes for "up" letters.	5	4	3	2	1
10.	I can read and sign the numbers 1–29.	5	4	3	2	1
11.	I know how to use different strategies to ask for a sign.	5	4	3	2	1
12.	I know how to affirm/negate a sentence.	5	4	3	2	1
13.	I understand the role Gallaudet University plays in the Deaf community.	5	4	3	2	1
14.	I know the vocabulary covered in this unit.	5	4	3	2	1

Identities

  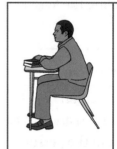 

identity of person living
in the Deaf world and
using American Sign
Language

describes a person who
hears and uses a spoken
language as their
primary language

Verbs

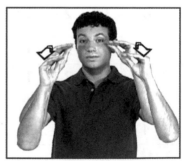

the act of instructing

the act of absorbing
information

Languages

"Good morning. My name is Mary. Thank you."

"Buenos días. Me llamo María. Gracias."

"Bon jour. Je máppelle Marie. Mercí."

Category Sign

Places of Learning

last few years of
secondary education,
i.e., Grades 9-12

a post-secondary
institution; college

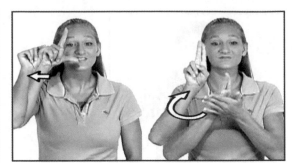

Gallaudet University

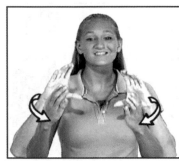

a group of students
in the same course

in that location; over
there

in this location; here

Responses

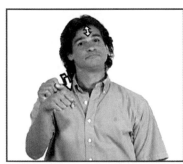

affirmative response

negative response

acknowledge
information

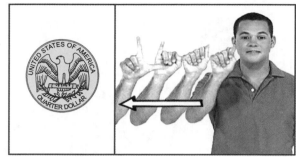

fingerspell: T-A-I-L

to begin a game;
to start

to have a victory;
to win

to not achieve a victory;
to lose

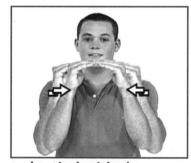

to be tied with the
opponent

Language Modality

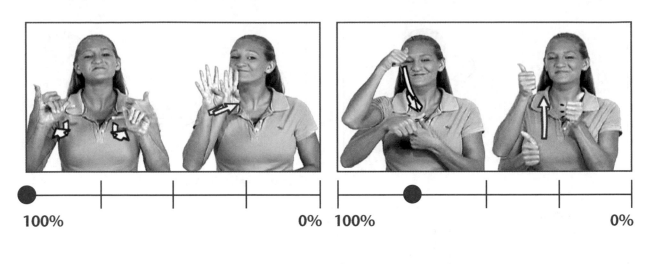

100% ———————————— 0%   100% ———————————— 0%

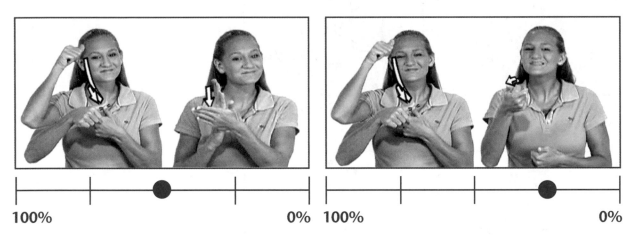

100% ———————————— 0%   100% ———————————— 0%

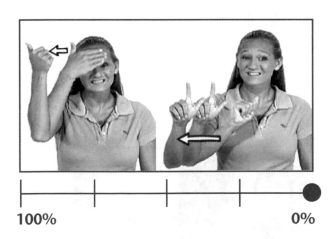

100% ———————————— 0%

Degree of Difficulty

very difficult   very easy

Other Signs

to be raised with, to grow up with; "all my life"

the equivalent of 12 months; year

The two of them together; both

Transition

presently; now

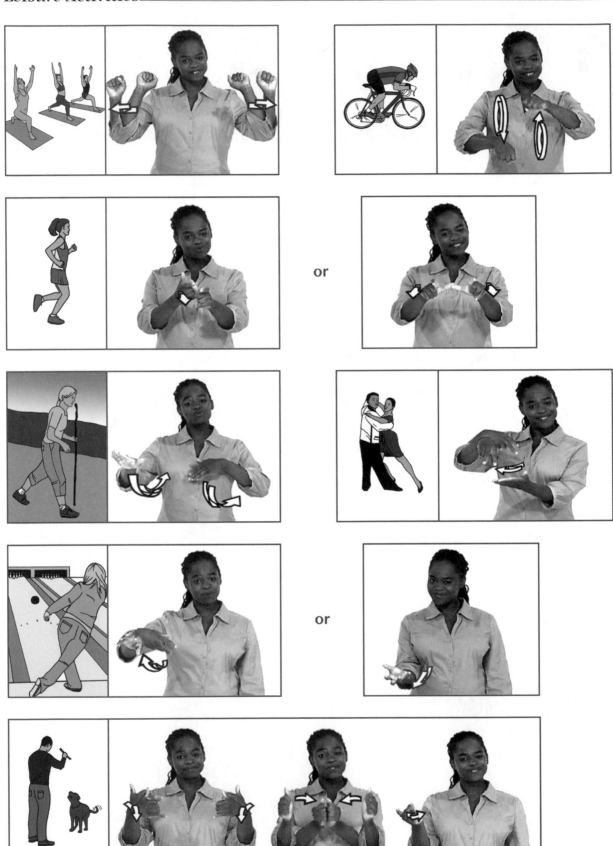

or

or

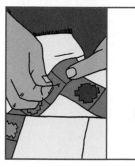

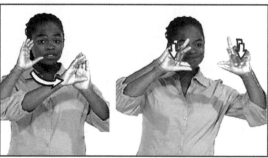

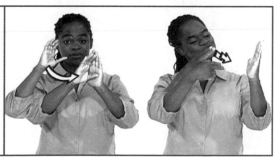

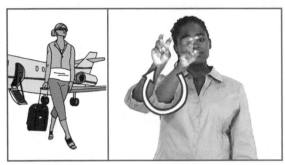

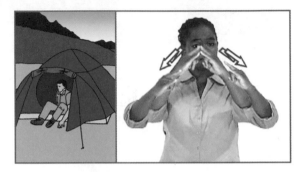

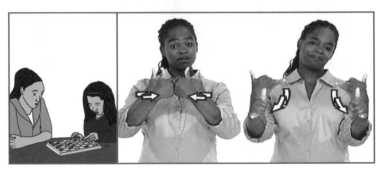

Actions

 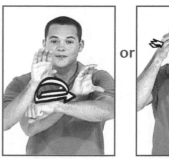 

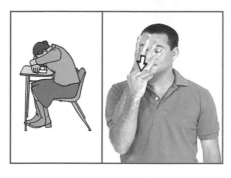  

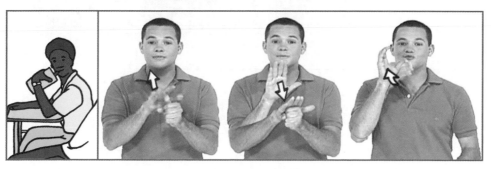

Degree of Attentiveness

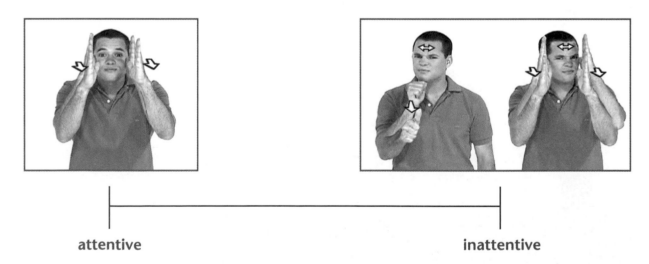

attentive   inattentive

Preferences

to detest; not like at all | to enjoy something; to like | to favor something; to prefer something

Drinks

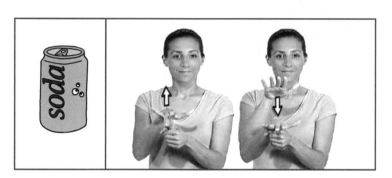

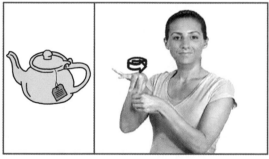

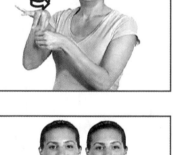 

Ask How One Is

ask how one is

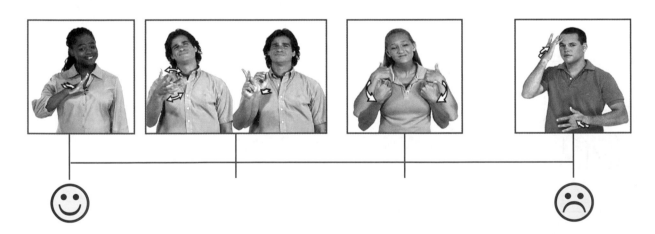

plus; add numbers in
an equation

minus; subtract numbers
in an equation

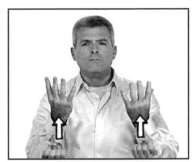

wh-word question:
ask how many

to possess, to own;
to have

zero

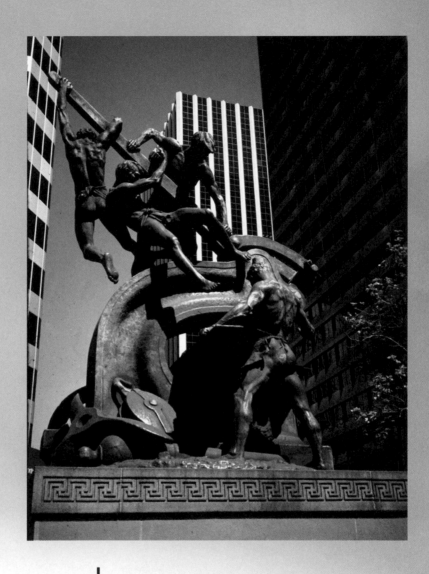

The Mechanics Douglas Tilden

"Labeled the Michelangelo of the West
for the vitality and energy of his sculpture,
Tilden's best known work is dedicated to
mechanics, particularly printing pressmen.
The sculpture presently stands at the
intersection of Market, Bush, and Battery
Streets in San Francisco.

-Deborah Meranski Sonnenstrahl,
Deaf Artists in America

UNIT 3

Discussing Living Situations

Homework 3:1

◉ CONVERSATION 1

Melinda (A) and Tyrone (B) demonstrate this dialogue in which they discuss where their homes are located.

> **Signer A:** Ask where B lives
> **Signer B:** Tell where (point in the direction of San Francisco)
> **A:** Ask B what area in the city
> **B:** Tell where it is (Golden Gate Park), ask A what area in the city she or he lives
> **A:** Respond (downtown)
> **A & B:** Discuss what they do in their areas

Key 🔑 Grammar

REAL WORLD ORIENTATION

Since ASL is a spatial language, when you tell where you live, you point in the direction where your home is located before giving the name of the city. You need to develop spatial awareness of your environment called "real world orientation." This includes learning where the different cities and areas of cities are located from where you are at that time. Use real world orientation to:
• point in the direction where your home is
• indicate the location where you are learning ASL
• refer to another person or object in the immediate environment.

To use this principle effectively, you should glance quickly in the direction in which you are pointing.

⊙ *Real World Orientation*

Tyrone demonstrates how to use "real world orientation" from Conversation 1. Notice how Tyrone glances as he points to the location.

⊙ MINIDIALOGUE

View the conversation between Ben and Joey. Then write in the information in the blanks below. The four cities mentioned are Berkeley, Fremont, Oakland, and San Francisco.

Berkeley: who lives there? _____

which area? _____

Fremont: who lives there? _____

which area? _____

Oakland: who lives there? _____

which area? _____

what can he see from his home? _____

What comment was made at the end of the conversation?

_____

Answers on page 407.

Vocabulary Review   Vocabulary covered in this lesson is on pages 156–159.

GIVING COMMANDS INVOLVING A LOCATION

In Unit 1, you learned how to give commands for actions involving the body, and for actions involving an object (Unit 1, page 30). Here, you learn to give commands involving a location.

When *giving commands involving a location*, follow the sequence below:

- name the location (raise brows)
- name the object (raise brows)
- indicate who (point to the person)
- give the command (to put the object in a specific place)

Remember to make your sign firmer and slightly bigger.

to put on a surface, i.e., shelf

to put in a container, i.e., box

 Commands 1–3

Michelle shows how to give commands for each action described below. See Michelle raise her brows when naming the location and the object before telling what to do.

Command 1 person putting an apple beside a wastebasket

Command 2 person putting coffee into a box

Command 3 person putting a backpack on the top shelf

Assignment Prepare two commands involving a location and an object to sign in class.

Vocabulary Review Vocabulary covered in this lesson is on pages 159–161.

DEAF PROFILE {

DOUGLAS TILDEN (1860–1935)

Called the Michelangelo of the American West, Douglas Tilden had roots in the vibrant and creative San Francisco Bay Area Deaf community, and was the first California sculptor to attain recognition and worldwide fame outside the U.S.

Tilden was born in 1860, in Chico, California, the second of five children. He became Deaf when he was four from a bout of scarlet fever. He entered the California School for the Deaf when he was five, and went home insisting that his parents, brothers, and sisters learned to sign.

After graduating from the California School of the Deaf in Berkeley, California in 1880, Tilden settled into a life teaching at the school. One day, he visited the studio of his brother, a sculptor. "What a wonderful world of new sensation," he later wrote. "It seemed to suffocate and intoxicate me... plaster casts of masterpieces, dead men's faces, busts, masses of white stone awaiting cutting... the smell of dampness, unswept floor, marble dust, delightful confusion."

Tilden began working with clay, but he knew he had to travel to Europe to grow as an artist. He traveled to Paris in 1888 and met his mentor, Paul Choppin, a famed sculptor who was also Deaf. When he exhibited his work at the salon there, his extraordinary sculptures attained wide-reaching celebrity. Tilden's artistic voice was uniquely capable—in his sculptures, one could feel the distinctive landscapes and the natural majesty of California. After eight years, he returned to California and was received by the community with praise. His work was exhibited along with work from Monet, Rembrandt, and Delacroix.

In 1889 he helped organize, and was voted vice president of the International Congress of the Deaf at its first convention in Paris. He proposed a bill to fight the rising tide of oralism, proclaiming at the convention, "Sign language is our language!"

As renowned as Tilden became, his interest in the rights and wellbeing of Deaf people was steadfast. While in Paris he became involved in the Deaf community that had blossomed around the Deaf school, and spent time in the Deaf club there. In 1889 he helped organize, and was voted vice president of the International Congress of the Deaf at its first convention in Paris. He proposed a bill to fight the rising tide of oralism, proclaiming at the convention, "Sign language is our language!" Tilden helped organize the California Association of the Deaf, drafting its constitution and bylaws.

When Tilden returned to California from Paris, James Duval Phelan, the wealthy mayor of San Francisco and later a United States Senator, became Tilden's patron. Phelan appointed Tilden to the city's beautification committee and commissioned him to create bronze statues to memorialize California. His enduring and famous works still stand in beauty and majesty in San Francisco and the surrounding Bay Area. Some of his best known works and their locations are: *Mechanics* (Market and Battery Streets, San Francisco); the *Football Players* (University of California Berkeley); the B*aseball Player;* and *Father Junipero Serra* (Golden Gate Park).

Many famous artists, writers, dancers, and politicians were regular visitors to his little studio in the west end of Berkeley. Tilden was a lively and well-read man, and San Francisco awaited his controversial articles in the daily newspapers. Later, in a time without interpreters or communication technology, he became an art professor at the University of California. When asked how he would communicate with his students, he said "I do not plan to talk to them, I plan to make them work."

Tilden is remembered in the art world as a standard-bearer for the spirit of the American West. In the Deaf community, he is remembered for his activism against the suppression of sign language for educating Deaf children. One of his most famous sculptures *The Bear Hunt* stands on the campus of the California School for the Deaf in Fremont. Tilden died of heart failure and was found dead in his studio in 1935.

Homework 3:4

MOVING LETTER "Z"

The letter "Z" is one of the two moving letters of the manual alphabet. The other letter is "J," which will be discussed later. Where the letter "Z" appears, in the beginning, in the middle, or at the end of a word, determines the hand position for the remaining letters.

Zip

When spelling a word with "Z" at the beginning, trace the letter "Z," hold the end position to spell the remaining letters. Observe how Cinnie fingerspells the word "zip."

Z . ip

Size

When spelling a word with "Z" in the middle, spell the letters before the "Z" in the normal fingerspelling hand position. After tracing "Z," hold the end position to spell the remaining letters. Observe how Cinnie fingerspells the word "size."

si . **Z** . e

Liz

When spelling a word with "Z" at the end, after tracing "Z," your hand position should be below the letters that preceded it. Observe how Cinnie fingerspells the name "Liz."

Li . **Z**

Words with "Z"

Tyrone and Melinda demonstrate how to fingerspell these words. Practice copying them.

"Z" in the beginning

Zelda

Zambia

Zit

Zebra

Zombie

"Z" in the middle

Suzy

Puzzle

Eliza

Seltzer

Bozo

"Z" at the end

Oz

Schmitz

Benz

Pez

Fizz

Write the Word

Tyrone and Melinda fingerspell words with "Z" in them.
Use the clues below to help you understand the words.
Write the words in the blanks.

1. (African nation/tribe) _____

2. (prestigious hotel) _____

3. (U.S. state) _____

4. (another name for Israel) _____

5. (female nickname) _____

6. (Starbucks name brand tea) _____

7. (branch of Buddhism) _____

8. (magician) _____

9. (clumsy) _____

10. (kind of hat) _____

11. (kind of jacket) _____

12. (measurement) _____

13. (reptile) _____

14. (labyrinth) _____

15. (habitat for animals) _____

16. (horoscope) _____

Answers on page 407.

Homework 3:5

CONVERSATION 2

Iva (A) and Michelle (B) demonstrate this dialogue in which they discuss their residences.

Signer	A:	Ask kind of residence B lives in
Signer	B:	Tell which kind
	A:	Ask about size
	B:	Reply
	A:	Ask if old or new
	B:	Tell which
	A:	Ask color of residence exterior
	B:	Tell color
	A:	Ask color of trim
	B:	Tell color
	A:	Ask if B likes the color
	B:	Give opinion
	A:	Respond
	B:	Ask A same questions about his/her residence
	A:	Reply

 **WH-WORD QUESTION—WHICH**

To ask a "which" question, use contrastive structure. For example, if you ask "Do you live in a house or an apartment?" place "house" and "apartment" in spaces opposite of each other. Then, ask the "which" question.

Contrastive Structure

See how Iva uses contrastive structure by nodding her head slightly and shifting her body from one side to the other. As a right-handed signer, she begins the contrastive structure on her left (her non-dominant side). She ends her question with the sign for "which" and furrowed brows.

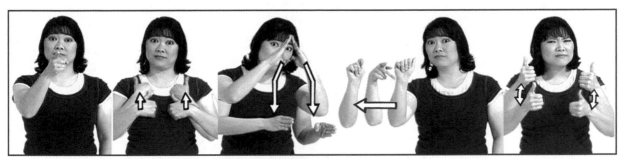

ask kind of residence one lives in

Sign Tip

Conveying Size

To indicate the size of something, use the following non-manual markers along with the sign.

this facial expression is used to indicate something is relatively small or smaller than expected

this facial expression is used to indicate something is average, ordinary, and/or comfortable size

this facial expression is used to indicate something is relatively larger than average size or larger than expected

⊙ MINIDIALOGUES

Watch the three minidialogues and answer the questions below. Observe the signers using contrastive structure.

Minidialogue 1

1. David uses contrastive structure to ask two questions. What are they?

2. Summarize the information given about Dale.

Minidialogue 2

1. Norman uses contrastive structure to ask two questions. What are they?

2. Summarize the information given about the Iva's residence.

Minidialogue 3

1. Cinnie uses contrastive structure to ask two questions. What are they?

2. Summarize the information given about Karen.

Answers given in class.

Vocabulary Review

Vocabulary covered in this lesson is on pages 161-163.

DID YOU REALIZE?

Diana, the popular royal Princess of Wales, acquired some fluency in British Sign Language (BSL) and raised awareness of BSL and Deaf people. She was the patron of the British Deaf Association (BDA) for 10 years, and was beloved and admired by the British Deaf community. She chose to sign her speech in BSL at the BDA's centennial celebration in 1990.

Homework 3:6

When objects are placed in an order, ordinal numbers are used, for example, "the first floor," "the second door," "the third drawer," or "the fourth shelf."

◉ ORDINAL NUMBERS 1ST–9TH

Watch how Iva signs numbers 1st–9th. As you sign the numbers 1st–9th, keep in mind the following:
• the number begins with the palm facing the side followed by a twist.

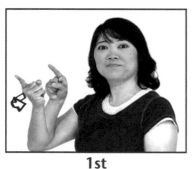
1st

4th

Sign Tip   These ordinal numbers are not used in ASL to say such things as "the first (time)..." or "First, you need..." Instead we use the sign:

the first (time)

GIVING BASIC DIRECTIONS

To give basic directions to a place, do the following:
- determine where the place is in relationship to where you are at the moment.
- establish a starting point (i.e., classroom door, or the main door)

 Giving Directions

Ben demonstrates how to give directions to three different locations.

On the same floor (telling where the lab is)
1. Ben begins by establishing the hallway.
2. Next, he gives the route to the lab along with non-manual markers to convey distance (see "conveying distance" below).
3. He tells which door is the lab with an ordinal number and raising his brows when indicating "that door."

On a different floor (telling where the men's restroom is)
1. Ben begins by telling it is upstairs, then giving the ordinal number for the floor (4th).
2. Then, he tells that the restroom is near the instructor's office.

In a different building (asking where the library is)
1. Ben begins by telling the person the library is in a different building.
2. Next, he tells the person to exit the building.
3. He indicates where the library is located using real world reference.

Observe how Ben raises his brows in the beginning of each demonstration when he names the location he will give directions to.

Conveying distance

You can indicate relative distance with specific non-manual markers—which show "far away," "moderate distance," or "very near/close."

far away

To indicate that a location is **far away**, do the following:

- tilt your head

- squint your eyes

- open your mouth slightly

- tell where: point with your arm fully extended

moderate distance

To indicate **moderate distance**, do the following:

- tilt your head

- purse your lips slightly

- tell where: point with your arm moderately extended

very near

To indicate that a location is **very near**, do the following:

- tilt your head

- clench teeth, turn head to the dominant side, with cheek almost touching shoulder

- tell where: point with your hand close to your body

Vocabulary Review

Vocabulary covered in this lesson is on pages 163–167.

Homework 3:7

IDENTIFY AND DRAW

This exercise gives you more practice taking the signer's perspective. Norman gives you instructions for what to do with the squares below. Norman identifies the squares and tells you what to put in them, beginning with an example.

		Example:

Answers are given in class.

Homework 3:8

CARDINAL NUMBERS 30–66

The numbers between 30 and 66 can be divided into three groups in terms of how they are signed.

Multiples of 10

Iva demonstrates the numbers 30, 40, 50, and 60.
Practice signing the numbers.
As you sign these numbers, keep in mind the following:

• 30, 40, and 50 start with 3, 4, or 5 facing out. Then the extended fingers and thumb close repeatedly.

• with 60, the thumb and pinky finger remain in contact while extended fingers close repeatedly.

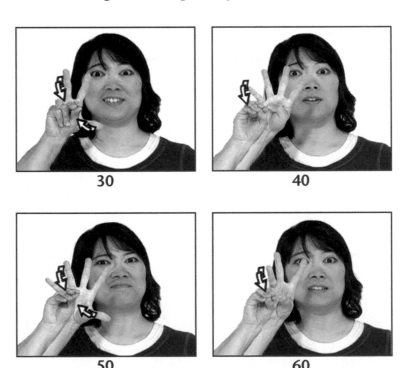

30   40

50   60

Multiples of 11

Iva demonstrates the numbers 33, 44, 55, and 66.

Practice signing the numbers.

As you sign these numbers, keep in mind the following:

- the palm faces down.
- those numbers are made with a "stamping" movement going sideways towards your dominant side.

33

44

55

66

Numbers 31–39

Iva demonstrates the numbers 31–39. Each number is shown from two angles–the front and the side. Practice signing the numbers.

As you sign these numbers, keep in mind the following:

- these numbers all slightly forward. Sign the first digit of the number with the palm facing out. The hand then moves slightly forward while signing the second digit. This is the same movement as you learned for numbers 23–29.
- for "31," when signing the "1," make sure the other fingers of the hand are closed in a fist, and not in a circle as in the letter "D."

NOTE: Numbers 41–49, 51–59, 61–65 are formed similarly to numbers 31–39. Begin with the first digit before your hand moves forward to sign the second digit in the number.

Write the Number

Write the number Joey gives.

1. _____	8. _____	15. _____
2. _____	9. _____	16. _____
3. _____	10. _____	17. _____
4. _____	11. _____	18. _____
5. _____	12. _____	19. _____
6. _____	13. _____	20. _____
7. _____	14. _____	

Answers on page 408.

How Many of What?

David and Joey use numbers between 30–66 in sentences.
Write the numbers and what they refer to.

number	refers to what?
1. _____	_____
2. _____	_____
3. _____	_____
4. _____	_____
5. _____	_____
6. _____	_____
7. _____	_____
8. _____	_____

Answers are given in class.

Homework 3:9

CONVERSATION 3

Norman (A) and Isias (B) demonstrate this dialogue in which they discuss their living arrangements as well as their teacher's. Notice when they summarize everybody's information, they orient their signs in the direction of the person they are talking about.

Signer A:	**Ask if B lives alone**
B:	**Reply**
A:	**Ask if B has a pet**
B:	**Respond**
	• size of pet(s)
	• color(s) and markings of pet(s)
	• name of pet(s)
A & B:	**Repeat dialogue** **(discuss A's and their teacher's living arrangements)**
A & B:	**Summarize information given about pets and living arrangements**

Key Grammar

SPATIAL AGREEMENT— ORIENTING SIGNS TO THE PERSON BEING REFERRED TO

In an earlier grammar note, you learned that, to show agreement, it is important to point to and glance at a person you are identifying. To continue to show agreement when sharing information about the person, orient your signs in the direction of the person you are talking about. For example, if you want to share information about yourself and a friend sitting on your right, information about yourself is signed directly in front of your body and information about your friend is signed slightly to the right of your body. To refer to people sitting across from you, sign the information further out in front of you to indicate the information is about the people across from you.

Orienting Signs

Isias and Norman demonstrate how to maintain spatial agreement by orienting their signs, bodies, and heads towards people being referred to:

• Isias tells what kind of and how many pets each person owns.

toward Norman

toward teacher

toward self

• Norman tells about each person's living arrangement.

toward Isias

toward teacher

toward self

Describing Pets

To describe your pets, follow this sequence:

1. tell what kind of pet: dog, cat, bird, etc.

2. indicate its relative size

- for large dogs, indicate the length and height (from the floor)
- for small dogs and remaining pets (cats, rats, rabbits, fish, turtles) indicate the length only in front of you
- for birds, indicate the height only, again in front of you.

3. use your body to describe the pet: main color and distinctive markings.

Sign Tip

Responding to yes-no questions

When you respond to a yes-no question, it is better to give more than a single "yes" or "no" response. For example, when giving an affirmative response to a question like "Do you live alone?" it is preferable and appropriate to say "Yes, I do live alone" than to simply say "Yes." Likewise, when giving a negative response to the above question, it is preferable to supply additional information, like "No, I live with my family" or "No, I live with my daughter" than to simply say "No." Answering "Yes" or "No" makes you appear as if you don't want to be bothered to answer and leaves the other person in the awkward position of feeling like they are prying. So make a habit of sharing information to help the conversation move along.

> **DID YOU REALIZE?**
>
> In the dialogue, Isias mentions that it's common to find deaf Dalmatians. Additionally, dogs and cats with white fur and blue eyes are often deaf. If you have a deaf pet, try signing with them!

 **MINIDIALOGUES**

View the two minidialogues and answer the questions below.

Minidialogue 1

(Tyrone and Ben as "Ryan")

1. What does Ryan say about his living arrangement?

2. Summarize the information given about each person:

name: 1) _____ 2) _____ 3) _____

likes: _____ _____ _____

3. What does Ryan say about the house they live in?

Minidialogue 2

1. What is Ben's problem?

2. What does the pet look like?

3. What does Michelle suggest that Ben do?

Answers are given in class.

Vocabulary Review Vocabulary covered in this lesson is on pages 167–170.

Homework 3:10

 EXPRESSING NEEDS

In these minidialogues, the signers express their needs and ask
where something is. View them and answer the questions below.

Minidialogue 1

1. What need is expressed?

2. What information is given?

Minidialogue 2

1. What need is expressed?

2. What information is given?

Minidialogue 3
1. What need is expressed?

2. What information is given?

3. What does Joey ask Melinda to do?

Answers given in class.

Responding to "Thank you"

As you may notice with examples from these minidialogues, the responses to "Thank you " are more similar to the Spanish "da nada" ("it's nothing") than to the English "You're welcome."

Priscilla's response to "Thank you"

Melinda's response to "Thank you"

Ben's response to "Thank you"

Vocabulary Review   Vocabulary covered in this lesson is on pages 170–171.

"THE ELEVATOR INCIDENT" BY MELINDA

View the story, then answer the questions below.

1. What does Melinda need to do?

2. Whom does she ask for assistance?

3. What happens the first time she goes up the elevator?

4. On her third attempt, what does Melinda ask the receptionist to do?

5. What happens when they get to the 4th floor?

6. How does Melinda react?

Answers given in class.

Vocabulary Review   Vocabulary covered in this lesson is on page 171.

Homework 3:11

"DOWN" LETTERS

The letters "Y," "Q," and "P" are made with the palm oriented downwards.

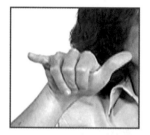

The letter "Y"

Notice as Cinnie fingerspells these words, her palm is oriented down when the letter "Y" is spelled.

    toy   merry   cyst

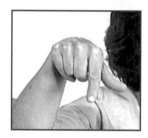

The letter "Q"

Again, as Cinnie fingerspells these words, notice her palm is oriented down when the letter "Q" is spelled.

    quiz   lacquer   BBQ (barbecue)

The letter "P"

As Cinnie fingerspells these words, notice her palm is oriented down when the letter "P" is spelled.

    nap   Patty

The letter "P" followed by "R" or "L"

As Cinnie fingerspells these words where the letter "P" is followed by "R" or "L," notice her palm is oriented down and tilted slightly sideways.

    Priscilla   plastic

Order the Words

For each category below, Melinda and Tyrone spell words in random order. Write the number next to the word.

Names

___ Paul	___ Kyle	___ Maya
___ Mary	___ Yoon	___ Lynn
___ Ryan		

More Names

___ Quinn	___ Yolanda	___ Evelyn
___ Lydia	___ Taylor	___ Peter
___ Priscilla		

Places

___ Quebec	___ Sydney
___ Quizno's	___ Quiche shop
___ Plaza	___ Baker's Square

Sign Tip

This sign represents the possessive "'s" in titles or names of stores.

Things

___ puppy	___ plywood	___ prize	___ quartz

More Things

___ map	___ onyx	___ yarn
___ quilt	___ yen	

Challenge Yourself

Take a blank sheet of paper and play each segment again. Look only at Melinda's and Tyrone's face, not their hands as they spell the words and write the words.

Answers on page 408.

Crossword Puzzle

Cinnie spells seven words and tells you where to place them in the grid below. The first word is filled in: You fill in the rest. Remember to take the signer's perspective.

		P									
		L									
		A									
		Z									
		A									

Answers on page 409.

Homework 3:12

LENGTHS OF TIME

Minutes 1–9

When specifying a length of time under 10 minutes, the numbers 1–9 are incorporated into the sign for "minute." Iva demonstrates 1–9 minutes.

| a minute, one minute | two minutes | three minutes |

10 Minutes

For "10 minutes," the number "10" is either incorporated into the sign for minutes (see the first example below), or the number "10" is given, followed by the sign for "minute." (see the second example below). Iva demonstrates both variations of "10 minutes."

 or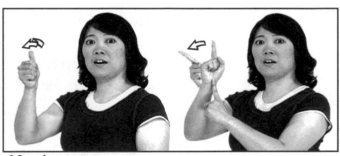

10 minutes   10 minutes

11 Minutes or Longer

For 11 minutes or longer, the number is not incorporated; instead, the number is given, followed by the sign for "minute." Iva demonstrates "11, 15, and 20 minutes."

11 minutes

15 minutes

20 minutes

Hours 1–9

When specifying a length of time under 10 hours, the numbers 1–9 are incorporated into the sign for "hour." Iva demonstrates the two forms for 1–9 hours from two angles.

an hour, 1 hour

2 hours

9 hours

⊙ 10 Hours or Longer

For "10 hours" or longer, the number is not incorporated into the hour sign; instead, the number is given, followed by the sign for "hour." Iva demonstrates "10, 12, and 24 hours" from two angles.

10 hours

12 hours

24 hours

HOW LONG DOES IT TAKE?

Here are two ways to ask "length of time" wh-word questions.

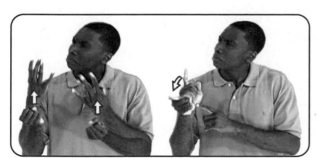

ask how many minutes it takes

ask how many hours it takes

In these minidialogues, one person asks how long it takes to do an activity. In the blanks below, write down the activity and the amount of time given,

	activity	**amount of time**		
Minidialogue 1:	_____	_____	Minute	Hour
Minidialogue 2:	_____	_____	Minute	Hour
Minidialogue 3:	_____	_____	Minute	Hour
Minidialogue 4:	_____	_____	Minute	Hour
Minidialogue 5:	_____	_____	Minute	Hour
Minidialogue 6:	_____	_____	Minute	Hour
Minidialogue 7:	_____	_____	Minute	Hour
Minidialogue 8:	_____	_____	Minute	Hour
Minidialogue 9:	_____	_____	Minute	Hour
Minidialogue 10:	_____	_____	Minute	Hour

Answers are given in class.

New Signs

These new signs appeared in the preceding minidialogues. Play the video again and see if you can determine the meaning of each sign listed. Give your answer by drawing a picture or writing a definition.

Minidialogue 3:

_____

Minidialogue 4:

_____

Minidialogue 7:

_____

Minidialogue 8:

_____

Minidialogues 6, 7 and 10:

_____

Minidialogue 10:

_____

Answers on page 409.

Homework 3:13

 CONVERSATION 4

Ben (A) and Michelle (B) demonstrate this dialogue in which they modify the movement of verbs to agree with the established locations of the places being discussed.

> **Signer A:** Ask where B works
> **Signer B:** Tell where (point)
> **A:** Confirm B lives in a certain city
> **B:** Confirm
> **A:** Ask how B goes to work
> **B:** Tell how
> **A:** Ask how long it takes to get from home to work (spatial agreement)
> **B:** Reply
> **A:** Give opinion about how long it takes
> **B:** Respond
> **A:** Ask if B comes to class from work (spatial agreement)
> **B:** Reply (negative, explain)
> **A:** Ask how B comes to class from home
> **B:** Reply
> **A:** Respond

Key Grammar

SPATIAL AGREEMENT—MODIFYING VERB MOVEMENT

Earlier, you learned how to use "real world orientation" to refer to the actual locations of your residence (city or area) (see page 3). Here, you learn to tell how to get from place to place (your home, your work place, and your class), and to tell how long it takes. The movement in these verbs below reflect the base forms, but when you are referring to established locations, the movement of the verbs is modified to show agreement with the location(s).

to go to...

to come here

When you want to ask how one goes from home to work, or how long it takes from work to class, you use real world orientation to refer to those locations and start in the direction of the home (or work), and end in the direction of the work place (or class).

MODIFYING VERB MOVEMENT

Ben and Michelle demonstrate the modified form of the verb "to come from home to here" to to agree with the two locations in this conversational exchange:

• when Ben asks Michelle how she comes to class
• Michelle replying how she comes to class and how long it takes

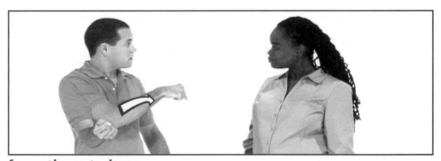
from there to here

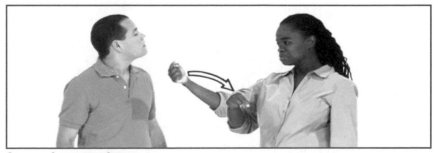
from there to here

Vocabulary Review   Vocabulary covered in this lesson is on pages 172-173.

Information about Another Person

Isias and Priscilla each give information about a person. Write the information in the spaces below.

Narrative 1 (Isias)

Name: _____

Lives in (city): _____

Near/area: _____

Type of residence: _____ size: _____

How long have they lived there: _____

Live with: _____

Pets (type, how many): _____

Work (place, how long): _____

How do they get to work: _____

How long it takes to get to work from home: _____

How do they get to class: _____

How long does it take to get to class: _____

Narrative 2 (Priscilla)

Name: _____

Lives in (city): _____

Near/area: _____

Type of residence: _____ size: _____

How long have they lived there: _____

Live with: _____

Pets (type, how many): _____

Work (place, how long): _____

How do they get to work: _____

How long it takes to get to work from home: _____

How do they get to class: _____

How long does it take to get to class: _____

Answers on page 410.

Your Narrative

Fill in the narrative guide with information from your own life. Use narratives by Isias and Priscilla as models to prepare yours. Rehearse until you no longer need to look at your notes. Remember to raise your brows to signal each transition. Prepare to present your narrative in the next class.

Name: _____

Live in (city): _____

Near/area: _____(optional)

Type of residence: _____ size: _____

How long have you lived there: _____

Live with: _____

Pets (type, how many): _____

Work (place, how long): _____

How do you get to work: _____

How long it takes to get to work from home: _____

How do you get to class: _____

How long does it take to get to class: _____

Homework 3:14

CULTURAL **VISUAL WAY OF LIVING**

Deaf people are visual beings and their vision is generally more acute. There is an expanding body of information about Deaf people's visual ways of living, including Deaf-friendly environments, or Deaf Space. Ideal environments for Deaf people have open spaces. The ideal floor plan in a Deaf-friendly house is visually open with walls that do not block views or present barriers to communication. Lighting is bright enough for easy visibility, but not glaring, or positioned in a way that makes it difficult to see the signer. Seating in a room is arranged to make sure people can see each other easily and also keep the door in sight. Mirrors are strategically placed to make obstructed parts of rooms visible, or to see who is approaching from behind.

Video phones and computers with web cameras are often integrated into areas where everyday life happens-in the kitchen or living room as opposed to being tucked away in an office. Alerting systems are visible, with lights whose flashing signals the doorbell or the phone ringing, or a baby crying in another room.

As more is known about living visually, Deaf friendly environments have become part of plans for the future. Gallaudet University is incorporating information from its Deaf Space Project into future building plans for the university. This includes more open buildings with fewer walls and appropriate lighting, and wider walkways throughout campus to ensure comfortable communication in ASL while walking from place to place. Deaf-friendly concepts are finding wider and wider application in classrooms, offices, senior citizen residence facilities, some neighborhoods, and even towns.

Homework 3:15

ASKING WHAT IS THE SIGN

Review strategies to ask for a sign you either don't know or have forgotten (See Unit 2, pages 84–86).

In each minidialogue, watch and identify one of the five strategies used to describe the objects or concepts below. Write the number of the strategy used in the box.

Strategy 1. point to object   **Strategy 4.** use opposites
Strategy 2. draw a picture   **Strategy 5.** describe/act out
Strategy 3. list things in the category

Minidialogue 1	Minidialogue 2	Minidialogue 3
Strategy #	Strategy #	Strategy #

Minidialogue 4	Minidialogue 5	Minidialogue 6
Strategy #	Strategy #	Strategy #

Answers are given in class.

Homework 3:16

 **CULTURAL**

SPEAKING IN THE PRESENCE OF A DEAF PERSON IS CONSIDERED IMPOLITE

At Deaf gatherings, Deaf schools, Deaf events, or other Deaf environments, people who know ASL at any skill level (even new students!) show courtesy and respect by signing to the best of their ability. In these Deaf spaces, if you know how to sign but speak instead, it is seen as inconsiderate. So remember to always sign in your ASL classroom, even before class or during a break.

If you are speaking with a non-signing person and a Deaf person comes in the room, it's commendable to serve as a bridge for both people, relaying the information to the Deaf person in between speaking to the non-signing person. Don't try to use your voice and sign at the same time as it compromises both languages, making for poor communication. So even if it takes a little longer, go ahead and relay the message using one language at a time. Your efforts will be appreciated.

UNIT 3 REVIEW

◉ QUESTIONS TO ASK

Now that you have reached the end of Unit 3, you should be able to ask the following questions. Read the cue for each question below, think about how you would sign it, and watch Stefanie sign the question on the DVD. Find a partner and practice signing the questions (and answers) to each other.

1. ask the person if s/he likes old or new cars

2. ask where the person lives

3. ask if the person lives alone

4. ask the person what kind of residence s/he lives in

5. ask the person if s/he has a pet

6. tell the person you need to see the teacher, ask where his/her office is located

7. ask the person how long it takes him/her to complete his/her homework

8. ask the person how s/he gets to class

9. ask the person if s/he knows the opposite of this sign:

10. ask the person to put the apple in the wastebasket

AUTOBIOGRAPHIES

Cinnie, Stefanie, and Tyrone assume the same characters from Autobiographies in Unit 2 and add more information about themselves. Summarize the information below.

Autobiography 1 (narrated by Cinnie)

Name _____

Personal information:

_____

_____

_____

_____

Autobiography 2 (narrated by Stefanie)

Name _____

Personal information:

_____

_____

_____

_____

Autobiography 3 (narrated by Tyrone)

Name _____

Personal information:

_____

_____

_____

_____

Answers on page 411.

SELF ASSESSMENT

Now that you are done with this unit, rate yourself using the list below: 5 being the most comfortable and confident you feel about your skill in the area and 1 being the least.

NOTE: If you marked 3 or below on any skill area, you should review that portion of the workbook.

1.	I know how to give commands involving objects and locations.	5	4	3	2	1
2.	I am able to correctly fingerspell words with the letter "Z."	5	4	3	2	1
3.	I know how to ask a "which" question using contrastive structure.	5	4	3	2	1
4.	I can read and sign correctly ordinal numbers 1st–9th.	5	4	3	2	1
5.	I know how to give directions to places on the same floor, different floor and/or different building.	5	4	3	2	1
6.	I know how to locate places using real world orientation.	5	4	3	2	1
7.	I know how to show spatial agreement by orienting sign to person I'm referring to.	5	4	3	2	1
8.	I know how to describe pets.	5	4	3	2	1
9.	I can use different strategies to ask for a sign.	5	4	3	2	1
10.	I know the correct number forms for cardinal numbers 1–66	5	4	3	2	1
11.	I know how to ask/tell how long something takes in minutes and hours.	5	4	3	2	1
12.	I know how to respond to "thank you."	5	4	3	2	1
13.	I am able to correctly fingerspell words with the letters "Y," "Q," and "P."	5	4	3	2	1
14.	I know how to modify verbs to show agreement with established locations.	5	4	3	2	1

Where One Resides

to reside; to live at

close by; in close proximity to

over there; in that direction

in this area; here

Cities

San Francisco

Oakland

Berkeley

Fremont

Write down the cities for your area that you learned in class:

city   **how to form the sign**

_____   _____

_____   _____

_____   _____

_____   _____

_____   _____

_____   _____

Category Sign

New York
Los Angeles
New Orleans
Chicago

Areas in a City

district, region, area

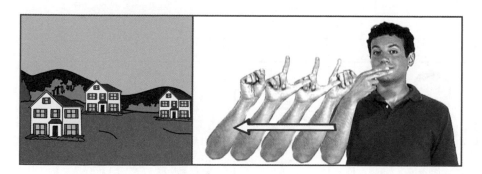

Compass Points

Locations

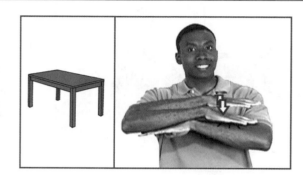

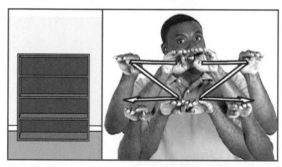

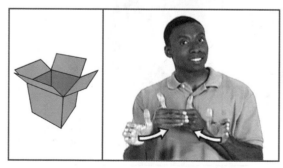

Objects

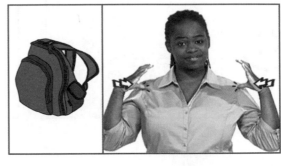

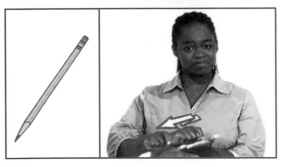

or

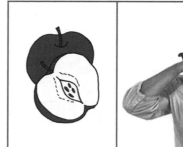

Action

to put something on a shelf, table, etc.

Types of Residence

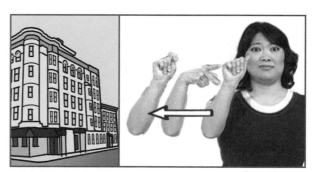

Size of Housing/Room

Age of Housing

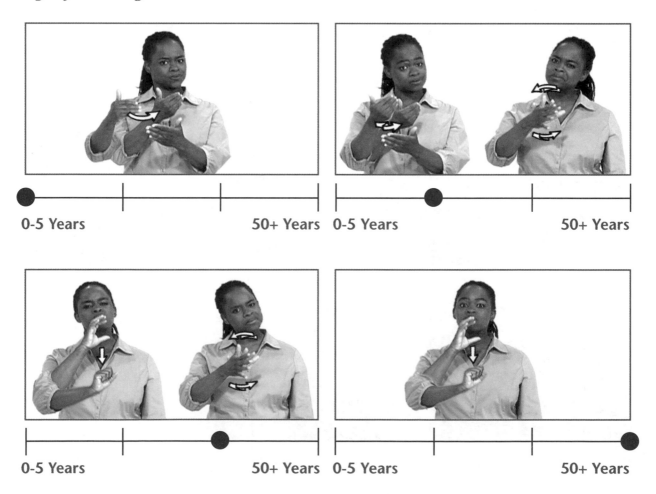

0-5 Years   50+ Years   0-5 Years   50+ Years

0-5 Years   50+ Years   0-5 Years   50+ Years

Wh-Word Question Signs

to ask which one

to ask what color

Facilities and Things

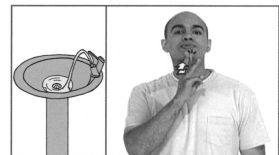

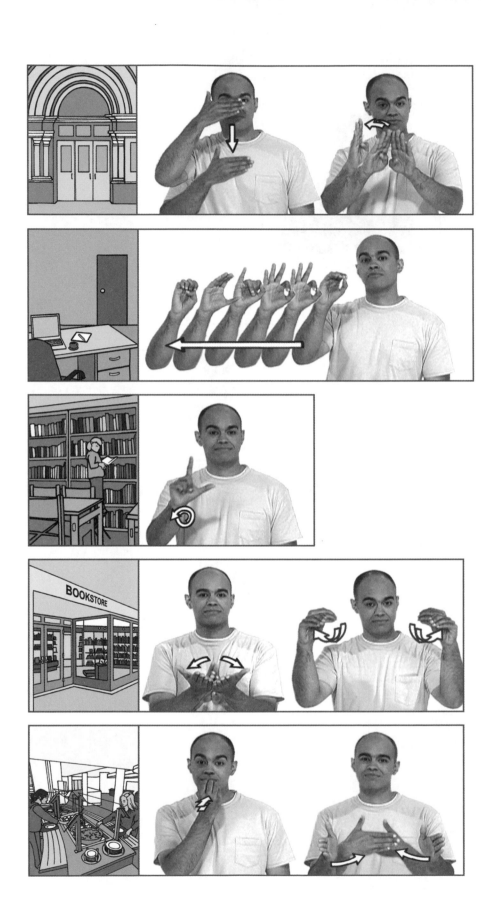

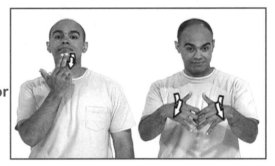

or

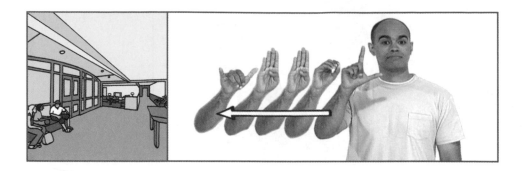

Category Sign

or

Giving Basic Directions

to go into; to enter

to go out; to exit

on the right side

on the left side

trace route

Living Arrangements

to live alone

to live with someone

a person(s) with whom one shares a residence; roommate

a male sweetheart; a boyfriend

a female sweetheart; a girlfriend

a social unit consisting of parents and children; a family

a male parent; father

a female parent; mother

a married man; male spouse; husband

a married woman; female spouse; wife

a male descendant; a son

a female descendant; a daughter

Category Signs

Pets

Category Signs

an animal living at one's home; pet

Discussing Possessions

to possess; to own

to have none of something

Expressing Needs

to need; should

to do repeatedly to be
proficient; to drill oneself

to purchase something

to put food in mouth;
to eat

to absorb liquid; to drink

to clean one's hands by
washing

Expressing Gratitude

express gratitude; "Thank you"

response to expression of gratitude

The Elevator Incident

to refrain with reluctance or discomfort

"come on," "hurry up"

to politely request; "please"

to be caught in an embarrassing situation; to feel like an idiot

"gotta go!" (to the bathroom)

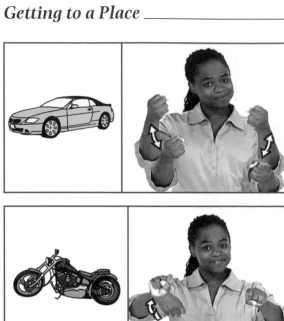

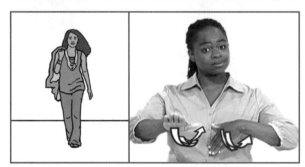

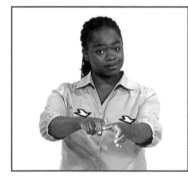

to ride in

to go someplace

to come here

Places

Frequency

all the time; always;
constantly

not at all; never

at times; sometimes

Wh-Word Question Signs

to ask how one does
something

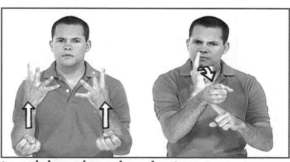

to ask how long in minutes

Ask How One Is: Response

to feel down

Signs from the Classroom

to be done with

to give instructions; to define; to describe

to put out of sight; conceal

to search; to look for

to uncover; find

to get someone to come here; to call someone here

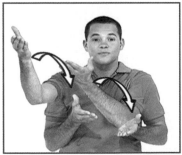

to deliver here; to bring here

Hearing Impaired: Wrong Way/ Deaf: Right Way

Ann Silver

"She uses street, parking, and warning signs as intermediaries to attract attention and to remove misconceptions about Deaf people that have been shaped by the educational and vocational rehabilitation systems..."

-Deborah Meranski Sonnenstrahl,
Deaf Artists in America

UNIT 4

Talking About Family

Homework 4:1

 ### CONVERSATION 1

Michelle (A) and Iva (B) demonstrate this dialogue in which they use contrastive structure to give information about children.

Signer A:	**Ask if B is married**
Signer B:	**Reply (negatively)**
A:	**Ask if B has a boyfriend**
B:	**Reply (affirmatively)**
A:	**Ask if B has children**
B:	**Reply (negatively)**
A:	**Ask if B wants to have children**
B:	**Tell desire for the future**
A:	**Respond**

 ### CONTRASTIVE STRUCTURE

In Unit 3, you learned to use contrastive structure to ask "which" questions. You can also use contrastive structure to compare and contrast two things by doing the following:

• establish one topic on your non-dominant side
• nod and shift your body slightly towards that side
• orient the signs about the topic towards that side
• then do the same for the other topic (usually the "opposite") on your dominant side.

Here contrastive structure is used to discuss the number of children a person has and whether they are boys or girls.

☉ *Contrastive Structure*

Iva demonstrates contrastive structure from Conversation 1 when stating she wants one boy (oriented on the left) and one girl (oriented on the right). This clip is in slow motion.

tells she desires one boy and one girl

☉ MINIDIALOGUES

Watch the three video minidialogues and answer the questions below. Observe the signers using contrastive structure.

Minidialogue 1

1. What does Tyrone compare/contrast?

2. How many more children does Anna want?

Minidialogue 2

1. What does David compare/contrast?

2. Where did David's sister meet her husband?

3. How long did they date?

4. When did they marry?

Minidialogue 3

1. What does Iva compare/contrast?

2. How many puppies look like their mother? Describe.

3. How many look like their father? Describe.

Answers are given in class.

Vocabulary Review Vocabulary covered in this lesson is on pages 216–219.

Homework 4:2

FORMING NEGATIVE RESPONSES

When asked a yes-no question that requires a negative response, begin with this sign, then give a negative statement.

**negative response
to yes-no question**

Depending on the type of question, use one of the following signs to make your negative statement. To respond negatively to questions like "Are you married?," or "Do you like ice cream?," use the sign below to state that something is not true or not correct. For example, "I'm not married," or "I don't like ice cream."

**stating something is
not true or not correct**

To respond to questions like "Do you have sisters?," or "Is there any more ice cream left?," use the sign below to state "I don't have any sisters," or "There is no ice cream left."

**stating one doesn't
have something**

Negative Responses. Melinda responds negatively to Ben's questions, first, about living with her parents, then about having Deaf siblings.

Remember to shake your head throughout a negative response.

Check the Response

Check the correct negative sign to use to respond to each question.

1. _____ _____

2. _____ _____

3. _____ _____

4. _____ _____

5. _____ _____

6. _____ _____

7. _____ _____

8. _____ _____

9. _____ _____

10. _____ _____

Answers on page 412.

Ways to Respond

As practiced in class, you can respond negatively to a yes-no question by:
- making a negative statement
- correcting the information
- or doing both of the above.

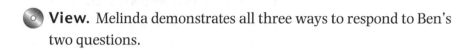 **View.** Melinda demonstrates all three ways to respond to Ben's two questions.

Vocabulary Review Vocabulary covered in this lesson is on page 219.

DID YOU REALIZE?

Deaf actors were free to play any role in the Silent Movies popular through the 1920s. Grandville Redmond, also a famous Deaf Artist appeared in eight Charlie Chaplin movies from 1918 to 1929. Redmond and Chaplin were close friends, and Redmond taught Chaplin Sign Language.

Homework 4:3

ROCKING NUMBERS 67–98

Several numbers between 67–98 require a twisting movement of the wrist. We call them "rocking numbers."

💿 *Numbers 67–89*

As you watch Iva demonstrate these numbers, observe the starting position and the twist movement associated. Iva demonstrates "67" again for left-handed signers.

67

68

69

78

79

89

💿 *Numbers 76–98*

As you watch Iva sign these numbers, observe the starting position and the twist movement. Iva demonstrates "76" again for left-handed signers.

76

86

87

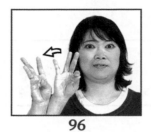
96

97

98

Identify the Number 1, 2, and 3

Joey signs one of the four numbers around him on the screen. Identify the number, then wait for the correct number to flash on the screen to see if you are correct.

1.

69   68

89   78

2.

87   76

86   98

3.

97   79

67   86

Challenge Yourself   Identify all numbers at fast forward (2x).

Circle the Number

1.	68	78	**6.**	87	97
2.	69	89	**7.**	79	89
3.	76	86	**8.**	98	87
4.	86	87	**9.**	69	97
5.	67	78	**10.**	68	86

Answers on page 412.

Write the Number

Each number is shown twice.

1. _____   5. _____   9. _____

2. _____   6. _____   10. _____

3. _____   7. _____   11. _____

4. _____   8. _____   12. _____

Answers are given in class.

Homework 4:4

DEAF PROFILE {

Philip worked selflessly for the rights of the Deaf community and for Deaf children and is remembered for her leadership, intelligence, and wit. She was a touchstone in a time of great change and achievement.

MARIE JEAN PHILIP (1953-1997)

Marie Jean Philip was a determined but gentle warrior in the fight to have Deaf children learn through ASL. At a critical time in Deaf Education and culture, she broke through boundaries and inspired change.

The oldest of three Deaf daughters born to Deaf parents, Philip went to the American School for the Deaf (ASD) in Hartford, Connecticut (the nation's first Deaf school, founded by Laurent Clerc and Thomas Gallaudet). Her parents taught her and her sisters to be independent and to think for themselves, telling their daughters that they could be whatever they wanted to be. By the time she was sixteen and a freshman at Gallaudet University, Philip had a strong conscience and a deep sense of love and respect for the Deaf community.

In her junior year, not even sure why she did so, she applied to attend Oberlin College as an exchange student. Her family and friends were stunned that she was prepared to go a year without being surrounded by sign language or Deaf people. When she arrived at Oberlin, she was immersed for the first time among hearing people, with no interpreters for classes and only a few classmates who knew a bit of fingerspelling. The experience gave her a positive, open view of people that would show through her actions all her life. She later remembered, "I knew I would be scared to come to a hearing college; I didn't realize that they were scared, too... I came to understand we're all human. That changed my perspective of hearing people." As would happen often in her interaction with people, several of her classmates at Oberlin went on to learn ASL and work with Deaf people after college.

In 1974, Philip became a research assistant at Northeastern University focusing on ASL, eventually teaching college-level ASL at Northeastern, Harvard University, and the Massachusetts Institute of Technology. She was an early advocate for ASL as a recognized language, and began spreading the word in the early 1980s. She brought this message not only to her home state, but also raised awareness on a national and international level through her workshops, speaking engagements, and at any other opportunity, even one-on-one.

The Learning Center for Deaf Children (TLC) changed its educational approach in 1985, looking to Philip to offer her vision and help put it in place. TLC became the first public school in the country to formally recognize ASL as the language of instruction. Within two years, Philip accepted a full time position as the Bilingual Bicultural Coordinator, and refined and expanded the educational and instructional environment. TLC and Philip became a beacon for those doubtful if an ASL-written English curriculum, which faced much public misunderstanding, was possible.

She took this awareness and willingness to push for change to a wider level, serving on a State of Massachusetts taskforce on Deafness that studied state departments and whether they met the needs of Deaf citizens. After the task force submitted the report, a bill was introduced in the State Legislature to set up a State Commission for the Deaf. Philip and the other Deaf advocates fought hard to lobby the legislators, and the Commission for Deafness was passed into law, and the commission established in 1986. Marie was also active in the Massachusetts State Association for the Deaf and served on the board of D.E.A.F., Inc., a service agency, for many years.

Philip was also a trailblazer in the field of Deaf culture. She was candid about the culture she loved, and fearless about sharing information or even challenging "icons" in the community to defend her principles and the value of her community's way of being. She brought cultural discussions to the forefront, on a national and international level, in a way that was unprecedented at the time. Scholars, researchers, and teachers knew they could rely on her for honest feedback, and she is thanked and acknowledged in countless seminal works on ASL and Deaf culture.

She was a strong advocate for Deaf people in other countries, and traveled all over the world. She was adept in International Sign Language and was in demand as an interpreter at international Deaf conferences and summits. Philip's community connection was deep and strong, from her lifetime ties to the Worcester Deaf Club near her home, to her tireless advice and assistance to those researching, teaching, and writing about ASL. Her work with the Deaf World was cut short when she passed away unexpectedly in 1997. Community leaders, colleagues, and friends attended her memorial, with people flying in from all of the world from countries such as Brazil, Japan, and Nicaragua.

Philip broke new ground in bilingual bicultural education, using ASL to teach children written English. The Learning Center named their new elementary school The Marie Jean Philip School in 2001. Her flair for storytelling and her contribution to culture is also commemorated with the annual Marie Jean Philip ASL Poetry, Storytelling, and Deaf Art competition, started in 1997.

Philip worked selflessly for the rights of the Deaf community and for Deaf children and is remembered for her leadership, intelligence, and wit. She was a touchstone in a time of great change and achievement. Her honest and compassionate approach to life won her admirers all over the globe and her presence is still missed.

SIGNING NATURALLY

Homework 4:5

⊙ CONVERSATION 2

Norman (A) and Stefanie (B) demonstrate this dialogue in which they use ranking to discuss siblings.

> **Signer A:** Ask if B has brothers or sisters
> **Signer B:** Respond
> **A:** Ask if B is the oldest
> **B:** Reply (use ranking)
> **A:** Ask about being close to a sibling
> **B:** Reply
> **A:** Ask about similarities and differences between B and that sibling
> **B:** Explain 2 of each
> **A:** Comment

Key Grammar

RANKING

Ranking, as seen in this conversation, establishes Stefanie as the second oldest of four children. Later in the conversation, ranking is used again to refer to the sibling to whom Stefanie is closest (the oldest). With ranking, the fingers of the non-dominant hand represent the total number of siblings in birth order. When referring to a particular sibling, or oneself, the signer points to the corresponding finger.

To indicate your ranking among siblings, do the following:
• first, use contrastive structure to tell the number of brothers and sisters
• then use fingers on your non-dominant hand to represent each sibling in their birth order
• point to the finger that represent you to give your ranking

View. Stefanie demonstrates ways to show ranking or birth order in families.

Only Child
If you are an only child, ranking is not needed. Use this sign that Stefanie demonstrates.

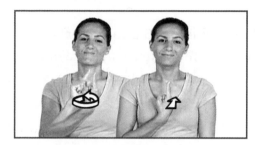

One Sibling
Instead of using ranking, just indicate you have a brother or sister and tell who is the oldest. Use the sign that Stefanie demonstrates in these two examples:

One Sibling 1. In this example, Stefanie is the oldest.
One Sibling 2. In this example, Stefanie's sister is the oldest.

Two Siblings (3 altogether)
You and your two siblings are represented with a "3" signed on the non-dominant hand. Point to a finger (or thumb) to indicate your ranking.

In this example, Stefanie is the youngest child out of three.

Three Siblings (4 altogether)

You and your three siblings are represented with a "4" signed on the non-dominant hand. Again, point to a finger to indicate your ranking.

In this example, Stefanie is the third oldest out of four.

Four Siblings (5 altogether)

You and your four siblings are represented with a "5" signed on the non-dominant hand. Again, you point to a finger (or thumb) to indicate your ranking.

In this example, Stefanie is the third oldest out of five.

Five Siblings (6 altogether)

When there are six children altogether and you are one of the oldest five, use the "5" hand on your non-dominant hand and point to a finger (or thumb) to tell your ranking. If you are the sixth child, tell you are the last one and use the ordinal number 6th to indicate ranking.

Five Siblings 1. In this example, Stefanie is the fifth child.
Five Siblings 2. In this example, Stefanie is the youngest (6th).

If you have more than five brothers and sisters, use an ordinal number to indicate your ranking. To review ordinal numbers, see Unit 3, page 122.

◉ MINIDIALOGUES

Watch the signers talk about ranking among siblings. Observe the use of the non-dominant hand to represent the number of siblings and to indicate ranking.

Minidialogue 1

1. How many brothers and sisters does Tyrone have?

2. What are their ages?

3. Explain their relationship.

Minidialogue 2

1. How many brothers and sisters does Michelle have?

2. Summarize the information given about each sibling (including Michelle's information).

3. Describe the two brothers' signing skills.

Minidialogue 3

1. What is Priscilla's rank in the family?

2. What are the ages of the siblings?

       1. _____   4. _____

       2. _____   5. _____

       3._____   6. _____

3. Which siblings are twins?

4. Describe how the twins are similar/different.

Answers are given in class.

Vocabulary Review   Vocabulary covered in this lesson is on page 220-221.

*"My Family" by Iva**

Iva signs a narrative about getting pregnant with her first child, and feeling pretty certain the baby will be Deaf because of the generations of family members being deaf on her side. When she gave birth to a daughter, she was surprised the baby was hearing. She then realized it was her husband who passed on the hearing gene.

Challenge Yourself   Learn to re-tell the story. Review the story until you can remember all the information. Then practice signing the information.

---

* This story is based on the life of Mary Hill Telford. Iva assumes her character and tells the story in the first person.

Homework 4:6

MOVING LETTER "J"

"J" is the other moving letter of the manual alphabet, the other being "Z" (Unit 3, page 115.) Because "J" is a moving letter, it influences the hand position of the letter that follows.

For names beginning with **"JA", "JE", "JO,"** the second letter (a, e. o) is embedded into the final position of the letter "J."

"A" (after "J")

"E" (after "J")

"O" (after "J")

For "**JU**," and "**JI**," the second letter "u" and "i" are also formed at the final position of the letter "J" and held as the hand rotates and faces forward.

"U" (after "J")

"I" (after "J")

🔘 **View.** Cinnie demonstrates how these letter combinations with "J" are formed: "Ja," "Je," "Jo," "Ju," and "Ji."

🔘 *Practice*

Melinda spells the names twice, first in slow motion, then at normal speed. Practice the movement used to spell names with the letter "J."

"JA"	"JE"	"JO"	"JU"	"JI"
JAY	JEAN	JOY	JUDY	JILL
JANE	JEFF	JOE	JULIET	JIM
JADE	JENNY	JOAN	JUTTA	JIRO
JACOB	JESSICA	JORDAN	JUNE	JIVIN

Pair Up. With a partner, take turns fingerspelling the names listed above. Follow this dialogue:

Signer A:	Spell a name from the list
Signer B:	Spell the name back to your partner
A:	Confirm or correct
B:	Put a check by the name

Homework 4:7

TELLING AGES

When giving the age of a person, the number is blended with the sign for "old." It starts with the index finger contacting the chin and moves outward.

 1–5 Years Old

Iva demonstrates the form for "1–5 years old." For these age signs, the palm faces out (instead of in like the cardinal numbers 1–5).

3 years old

 6–9 Years Old

Iva demonstrates the form for "6–9 years old." Notice the palm faces out like the cardinal numbers 6–9 and the index finger contacts the chin before moving outward.

7 years old

10 Years Old

Iva demonstrates the form for "10 years old." Notice the first handshape is "L-shaped" with the index finger contacting the chin and becomes "10" as the hand moves outward.

10 years old

11–15 Years Old

Iva demonstrates the form for "11–15 years old." Notice her other fingers including the index finger make contact with the chin before moving outward to form the number.

12 years old

16–19 Years Old

Iva demonstrates the form for "16–19 years old." Notice the palm faces in and the index finger touches the chin with a "L" handshape and then the hand moves outward to tell "16–19 years old."

18 years old (begins with "L")

16–19 Years Old (variation)

Iva demonstrates a common variation to signing "16–19 years old" which begins with a "5" handshape.

18 years old (begins with "5")

20 Years Old and Older

Iva demonstrates this form using "41 and 55 years old." Notice the index finger of the first digit touches the chin and remains the same as the hand moves outward and then changes to the sign of the second digit at the end of the movement after a slight pause.

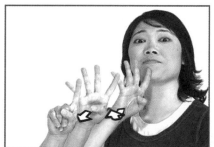

41 years old　　　　**55 years old**

Less than One Year Old

Iva demonstrates how to give age for under one year old. Notice the number is incorporated in the sign for "month," followed by the sign for "age or old."

4 months old

11 months old

How Old?

The signers sign statements with ages. Write down the age and circle the person or pet the age refers to.

age	whose age?		
1. _____	dog	cat	bird
2. _____	oldest brother	oldest son	oldest daughter
3. _____	baby	goldfish	rabbit
4. _____	son	daughter	sister
5. _____	roommate's son	son's roommate	son
6. _____	sister	son	daughter
7. _____	dog	cat	bird
8. _____	brother's oldest son	sister's oldest son	brother's oldest daughter
9. _____	son's baby	sister's baby	daughter's baby
10. _____	brother	brother-in-law	son
11. _____	I/me	wife	both of us
12. _____	mother	father	bird

Answers are given in class.

Identify Number Type

Isias and Melinda sign either an age or an ordinal number. Write down the number and circle the type of number—age or cardinal.

age			age		
1. _____	age	cardinal	11. _____	age	cardinal
2. _____	age	cardinal	12. _____	age	cardinal
3. _____	age	cardinal	13. _____	age	cardinal
4. _____	age	cardinal	14. _____	age	cardinal
5. _____	age	cardinal	15. _____	age	cardinal
6. _____	age	cardinal	16. _____	age	cardinal
7. _____	age	cardinal	17. _____	age	cardinal
8. _____	age	cardinal	18. _____	age	cardinal
9. _____	age	cardinal	19. _____	age	cardinal
10. _____	age	cardinal	20. _____	age	cardinal

Answers on page 413.

Homework 4:8

⊙ CONVERSATION 3

Isias (A) and Priscilla (B) demonstrate this dialogue in which they discuss their relatives using possessive adjectives.

> Signer A: Ask if B's mother has brothers and sisters
> Signer B: Respond, tell how many
> A: Ask if B's mother is the oldest
> B: Respond
> A: Ask if B's father has any brothers and sisters
> B: Respond, tell how many
> A: Ask if B's father is the oldest
> B: Respond
> A: Confirm the total number of aunts and uncles B has
> B: Confirm
> A: Ask if B has any cousins
> B: Respond, tell how many
> A: Comment, ask if B's grandparents are still living
> B: Reply

Key Grammar

POSSESSIVE ADJECTIVES

One way to discuss possessives in ASL is using *possessive adjectives*. In English, possessive adjectives like "your," "his," or "her" are used in sentences like "Your sister and *his* mother are the same woman," or "I saw *her* father yesterday." In ASL, possessive adjectives are made with a single movement of the "open B" hand followed by a noun. The "open B" hand is oriented toward the person who "owns" the person, place, or thing being discussed. Unlike possessive adjectives in English, ASL possessive adjectives do not reflect gender. Instead they indicate the location of the "owner."

Possessive Adjectives

Isias demonstrates a possessive adjective when asking you about your grandparents. Notice how he orients his "open B" hand toward you, the "owner."

ask if the person's grandparents are still living

MINIDIALOGUES

Watch the three minidialogues and answer the questions. Observe the signers discussing their relatives using possessive adjectives.

Minidialogue 1
1. Explain how the baby is related to Cinnie.

2. Which of Cinnie's children is the baby's parent?

3. Who will be attending the baby's one-year-old birthday party?

4. What will Cinnie give the baby?

Minidialogue 2

1. List who attended and did not attend the wedding.

2. Where did the couple meet?

3. How long had they dated?

4. What does David say about his wife's pregnancy?

5. What does David think of his in-laws?

Minidialogue 3

1. Whose cousin are they talking about? That cousin was thought to be what?

Did you catch Stefanie using this sign to respond to Isias?

2. How did the cousin learn to sign so well?

express amazement

3. What is the cousin's current living situation?

4. What is unique about the cat?

Answers are given in class.

Vocabulary Review   Vocabulary covered in this lesson is on pages 220–224.

Homework 4:9

💿 WHAT'S THE RELATIONSHIP?

Watch closely how Melinda and Michelle use possessive adjectives and personal pronouns to explain how people are related to them and to each other.

possessive adjective

personal pronoun

Write your answer to the questions.

1. _____

2. _____

3. _____

4. _____

5. _____

6. _____

7. _____

8. _____

Answers are given in class.

PRONOUNS AND POSSESSIVES

Translate these two sentences:

"*You're* a baby" and "*Your baby* is so cute!"

Yes, for the first sentence, you use the "index" hand, and for the other sentence, you use the "open B" hand. So before you translate sentences using personal pronouns and possessive adjectives, think about their handshapes and meaning. Otherwise, what you want to convey will be way off base!

Now, translate the sentences below into ASL using the appropriate personal pronouns and/or possessive adjectives.

a personal pronoun   a possessive adjective

1. My house is green. Your house is blue.

2. Your cat is brown.

3. You're not a rat.

4. I saw her mother in the library.

5. I found your glasses.

6. You're a student.

7. You're her friend.

8. I like her.

9. His children are here.

10. He's my sister's son.

11. His father is my uncle.

12. She lives in France. Her parents live in England.

Be prepared to sign the sentences in class.

Homework 4:10

QUESTION AFTER A NEGATIVE STATEMENT

Ben demonstrates making a negative statement using the sign below followed by a question.

stating one doesn't have something

Melinda demonstrates making another negative statement using the sign below followed by a question.

stating it is not true; or incorrect

Assignment You are to develop six negative statements followed by a question. Be prepared to sign them in class.

Homework 4:11

TEN YEARS LATER...

Melinda updates you about what happened to the family members pictured below in the past ten years. After each segment, write the information given. *Answers on page 413.*

Homework 4:12

◉ REVIEW NUMBERS 1–100

Joey signs the blocks of numbers shown below. Sign the numbers along with Joey.

1–19	**30–39**	**60–79**
20–29	**40–59**	**80–100**

To sign the number "100," keep your palm out and move your hand forward slightly when changing from "1" to a "C" handshape.

◉ *What Number Is It?*

Isias, Priscilla, and David ask what number comes before, after, or between given numbers. For example:

Example 1: Isias asks what number comes before 4

Example 2: Priscilla asks what number comes after 4

Example 3: David asks what number is between 3 and 5

Write the number.

1. _____	10. _____	19. _____
2. _____	11. _____	20. _____
3. _____	12. _____	21. _____
4. _____	13. _____	22. _____
5. _____	14. _____	23. _____
6. _____	15. _____	24. _____
7. _____	16. _____	25. _____
8. _____	17. _____	26. _____
9. _____	18. _____	27. _____

Answers on page 414.

Homework 4:13

💿 DAVID'S KEYS

View. David has lost his keys and, luckily, Iva found them. Watch this segment and answer the questions below.

1. How many keys does David have altogether? _____

2. What are the keys for, and how many does he have for each purpose?

for _____ how many? _____

for _____ how many? _____

for _____ how many? _____

for _____ how many? _____

for _____ how many? _____

for _____ how many? _____

for _____ how many? _____

3. Where did Iva find the keys? _____

4. In what city does David live? _____

Answers are given in class.

New signs:

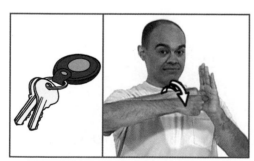

New York

to ask the purpose of

Vocabulary Review   These signs are also in vocabulary review on page 224.

Homework 4:14

 COMMENTING ON FAMILY MEMBERS

Watch the three video conversations and answer the questions below.

Minidialogue 1

1. What two comments does Stefanie make about Priscilla's grandmother?

2. How old is Priscilla's grandmother?

3. How does Priscilla explain her grandmother's youthful look?

4. To be like the grandmother, what do Priscilla and Stefanie both agree they should do?

Minidialogue 2

1. Why can't Iva pick out Melinda in the photo?

2. What is the story behind the good-looking guy in the photo?

3. Is Melinda married now? Explain.

4. What does Iva need to do now?

5. What does Melinda suggest Iva take with her to Mexico?

Minidialogue 3

1. When and where was the photo taken?

2. What was the occasion?

3. The photo consists of...?

4. Which child does Joey think looks like Cinnie? In what ways?

5. Does Joey have any grandchildren?

Answers are given in class.

Vocabulary Review Vocabulary covered in this lesson is on pages 224–227.

Homework 4:15

MAINTAINING A CLEAR SIGHTLINE

When several people are engaged in a conversation in ASL, it's best to sit in a circle so everyone can see or be seen. This creates "clear sightlines" between all of the signers in the group. However, when circumstances do not accommodate this arrangement, adjustments can be made so everyone has a clear view. The following video shows the responsibilities of group members to maintain clear sightlines.

The Signer

Position yourself so others can see you clearly. If the group is seated, you may need to lean forward a little. Sometimes you might have to stand up, or move to a place in front of the group.

Watch how Priscilla leans forward and checks to see if the sightline is clear.

The Listeners
In Between

Be conscious that in your need to see a signer next to you, you may be blocking someone else's view. Check to ensure the sightline is clear. Glance around quickly to gauge other's sightlines are clear. If needed, you may lean back without losing your own view. Sometimes moving your chair back helps ensure both you and others can see.

Watch how Norman leans back and checks to see if the sightline is clear.

At the End

Be assertive in adjusting yourself or informing others if you don't have a clear sightline of the signer. This is usually done by pressing the shoulder of the person blocking your view. First adjust your position. If this doesn't work, adjust the position of the person blocking your view by pressing their shoulder in the direction you want them to move. The person should change their position without needing to look at you. Remember, don't tap someone's shoulder unless you want to get his or her attention.

Watch Isias press Norman's shoulder, indicating Norman needs to lean back.

QUESTIONS TO ASK

Now that you have reached the end of Unit 4, you should be able to ask the following questions. Read the cue for each question, think about how you would ask it, and watch Norman sign the question on the video.

1. ask if the person is married.
2. ask if the person wants children in the future.
3. explain you have one brother and one sister and you are the baby in the family. Then, ask if the person has brothers and sisters.
4. ask if the person is the oldest (sibling).
5. ask if the person's sister is pregnant.
6. ask the person whom s/he is closest to.
7. ask the person how old s/he is.
8. tell which of your grandparents are living and which are not. Then ask if the person's grandparents are still living.
9. explain you have no nieces and nephews. Then ask if the person has any.
10. ask the person what the opposite of this sign is:

Find a partner and practice signing the questions and answers to each other.

 **AUTOBIOGRAPHIES**

Tyrone, Cinnie, and Stefanie add to Billy's, Emma's, and Sara's autobiographies. Summarize the information given.

Autobiography 1

Name _____

Personal information:

_____

_____

_____

_____

_____

_____

_____

_____

_____

_____

Autobiography 2

Name _____

Personal information:

_____

_____

_____

_____

_____

_____

_____

_____

_____

_____

_____

Autobiography 3

Name _____

Personal information:

_____

_____

_____

_____

_____

_____

_____

_____

_____

_____

Answers on pages 414–416.

SELF-ASSESSMENT

Now that you are done with this unit, rate yourself using the list below: 5 indicates feeling the most comfortable and confident about your skill in that area and 1 indicates feeling the least confident.

NOTE: If you marked 3 or below on any skill area, you should review that portion of the workbook.

1.	I am able to ask someone if they are married and then ask other personal questions about family.	5	4	3	2	1
2.	I am able to ask someone if they have siblings, who is the oldest, and ask about similarities and differences between siblings	5	4	3	2	1
3.	I can read and sign cardinal numbers 1–100	5	4	3	2	1
4.	I know the different hand positions when fingerspelling the letter "J."	5	4	3	2	1
5.	I know how to indicate one's rank among siblings when when discussing ages.	5	4	3	2	1
6.	I can read and sign age numbers.	5	4	3	2	1
7.	I know how to use possessive adjectives to tell or ask about people's relationships.	5	4	3	2	1
8.	I know how to give two different negative responses.	5	4	3	2	1
9.	I am able to make a negative statement, correct information, or do both.	5	4	3	2	1
10.	I am able to make negative statements and then ask follow up questions.	5	4	3	2	1
11.	I am able to ask someone yes-no questions regarding relatives and whether the relatives are still living or dead.	5	4	3	2	1
12.	I know to use different strategies to get my meaning across when I don't know a sign for it.	5	4	3	2	1
13.	I know to make complimentary comments to people about their families.	5	4	3	2	1
14.	I know how to maintain a clear sightline at all times, both as a signer and as a listener.	5	4	3	2	1
15.	I know the vocabulary used in this unit.	5	4	3	2	1

Gender

male; a male child;
a boy

female; a female child;
a girl

Immediate Family Members

a female parent; a mother

or

a male parent; a father

or

mother and father;
parents

a female offspring;
a daughter

a male offspring;
a son

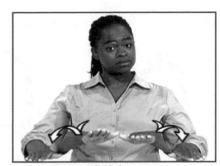

offspring; children

two born at the same
birth; twins

a female sibling;
a sister

a male sibling;
a brother

brothers and sisters; siblings

Category Sign

a unit consisting of
parents and children;
a family

Starting a Family

| to become pregnant; to conceive a child | to have offspring developing in the womb; to be with child | to give birth to a child |

Stages of Relationship

begin to experience feeling of love toward...; "fall in love with"

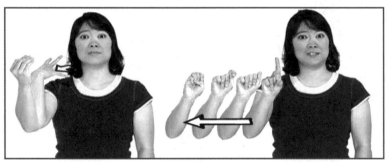

to take someone out for a romantic evening; to go on a date

to exclusively date one person

a male sweetheart; a boyfriend

a female sweetheart; a girlfriend

to propose marriage

to promise to marry;
betrothed; be engaged

to unite in wedlock;
to wed or marry

a male spouse;
a married man

a female spouse;
a married woman

Desire for the Future

in the future

to desire something

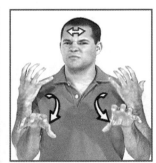

to not desire
something

perhaps, a
possibility of

Negative Responses

negative response
to yes-no question

stating it's not true
or incorrect

stating one doesn't
have something

Ranking ——————————————— *Plural Pronouns* ——————

first born among siblings; the oldest

the last born among siblings; the youngest

the two of you

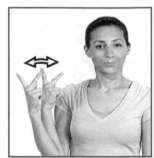

the two of us

Kind of Relationship—— *Comment*———— *Extended Family Members*——————

to have a strong bond, be close to

fascinating; interesting

the father of one's parent, a grandfather

the mother of one's parent, a grandmother

the son of one's child; a grandson

the daughter of one's child, a granddaughter

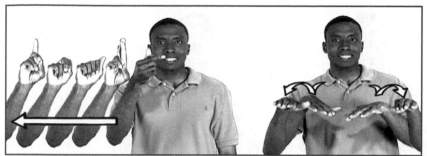

the children of one's child, grandchildren

a relative by marriage; "in law"

the sister of one's parent; an aunt

the brother of one's parents; an uncle

a sibling's daughter; a niece

a sibling's son; a nephew

uncles' and aunts' children; cousins

Aging

to age; to grow old

not dead; still alive

to stop living; to be dead

euphemism for being dead; cease to exist

the total number

Family Variations

mother's other husband; step father

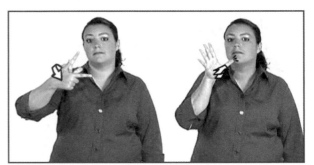

father's other wife; step mother

spouse's daughter from a previous marriage;
step daughter

a stepparent's son; step brother

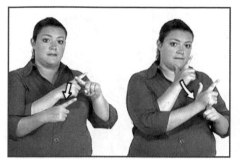

siblings who have one parent in common; half sister

siblings who have one parent in common; half brother

a committed life partner

Sexual Orientation

a man attracted to men; a gay man

a woman attracted to women; a lesbian

a person attracted to the opposite sex; "straight"

Changes in Relationship

to legally take a child into one's family; to adopt

to take responsibility for; to look after

a heated verbal argument; a falling out

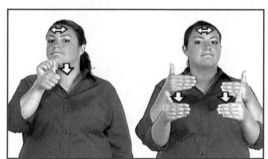

to not be on friendly terms; to not get along

love being on the wane; "fall out of love"

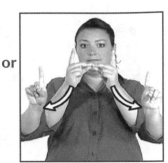

or

to part company; cease to associate

arrangement by which spouses live apart; to separate

legal dissolution of a marriage; a divorce

David's Keys

New York

to ask the purpose of

Occasions

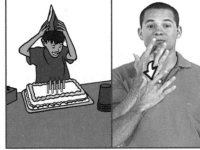

or

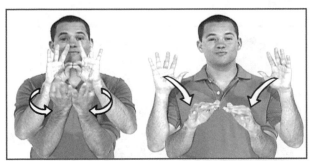

a gathering of relatives; a family reunion

or

or

time off from work or
school; a vacation

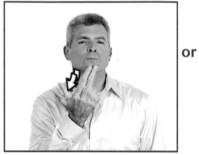 or

attractive or adorable, usually
refs to young people; "cute"

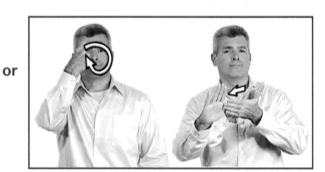

pleasing; attractive, usually
refers to females; "beautiful"

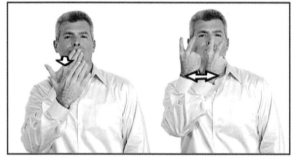 or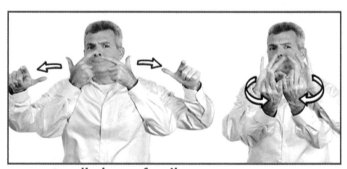

good looking; attractive, usually refers
to males; "handsome"

a pleasant, attractive, and/or
respectable family

an unusually large family

to share a resemblance with someone

to have a youthful look

to look differently than before

to show no change in appearance

Wh-Word Question Sign

to ask about age

"Buy me! I know **sign language**."

Buy Me, I Know Sign Language
Shawn Richardson

"...Richardson brings the "best friend" to new levels by showing that owner and pet speak the same language—a concept not limited to appearances."

-Deborah Meranski Sonnenstrahl,
Deaf Artists in America

UNIT 5

Telling about Activities

Homework 5:1

 CONVERSATION 1

Iva (A) and Priscilla (B) demonstrate this dialogue in which Iva begins by asking a wh-word question to find out when Priscilla exercised.

> **Signer A:** Ask when B did something (exercise)
> **B:** Tell when
> **A & B:** Discuss the activity

Key Grammar

WH-WORD QUESTION - WHEN

In English, a "when" question can be used to ask for either "what day" or "what time." In ASL, a "when" question can only be used to ask "what day."

To ask a "when" question, do the following:

1. name the activity
   • raise brows
2. ask "when"
   • lower brows
   • lean head forward
   • hold the last sign (the "when" question sign)

When Question

Iva demonstrates "ask when someone did something" from Conversation 1. Pay close attention to the word order and non-manual markers.

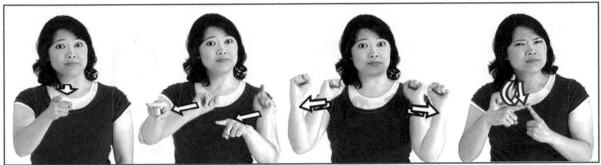

ask when person did something (exercise)

A SIGN OF CAUTION: If you wanted to know what time your friend planned to do an activity, make sure to use the sign at right.

ask what time

CONVERSATION 2

Norman (A) and Stefanie (B) demonstrate this dialogue in which Norman uses a different wh-word question to ask what Stefanie did recently.

Signer A:	Ask B what s/he did on a certain day (last Tuesday)
B:	Tell activity
A & B:	Discuss the activity

WH-WORD QUESTION—WHAT A PERSON DID/WILL DO

To ask a question about what a person did or will do on a particular day use the sign shown below. It can be signed with both hands or with one hand.

A SIGN OF CAUTION: These signs are used to ask questions only. They are not used in a statement. For example, do not use the sign to say the equivalent of "I'm doing my homework."

 or

(two hands)   (one hand)

To ask a "what one did/will do" question, do the following:

1. name the day
  • raise brows
2. ask what person did/will do
  • lower brows
  • lean head forward
  • hold the last sign (the "what did/will do" question sign)

💿 *What Did/Will Do Question*

Norman demonstrates "ask what person did/will do" from Conversation 2. Pay attention to the word order and non-manual markers.

ask what person did/will do on a certain day (last Tuesday)

ESTABLISH TENSE

Time signs usually occur at the beginning of a sentence to establish tense. All following events described are understood as occurring at that time.

If a time sign is not specified, then it is assumed that the events described are in the present tense.

Verbs in ASL are not modified specifically for tense like in some other languages. Hurrah! No conjugated verbs!

Time signs reflecting tense are on an imaginary time line like the one pictured below. Time signs referring to the future tend to move forward; time signs referring to the past tend to move back, and time signs referring to the present are usually signed right in front of the body.

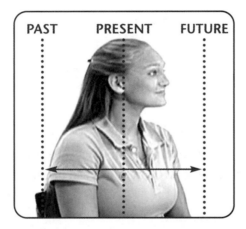

Below are examples of time signs that reflect points on the time line. Let's assume "today" is Wednesday.

the day before today; yesterday

last Monday, the past Monday

at the present time,
now, today

the day after "today,"
tomorrow

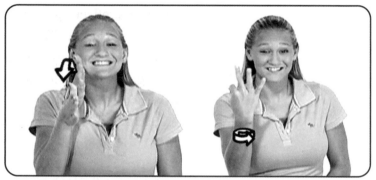

next Friday, this Friday

💿 MINIDIALOGUES

View the three video conversations and answer the questions
below. Observe how wh-word questions are asked.

Minidialogue 1

1. What does Michelle ask David?

2. What does David say he did and didn't do? Explain.

3. How is David doing now?

Minidialogue 2

1. What does Tyrone ask Ben? What is Ben's response?

2. What does Tyrone remind Ben to get?

3. What is Ben doing now?

4. Why doesn't Tyrone want to go with Ben?

Minidialogue 3 (Cinnie and Joey)

1. What does Cinnie ask Joey? What is Joey's response?

2. Why is Jack's name brought up?

3. How is Jack related to Cinnie?

4. What does Jack look like?

Answers are given in class.

Vocabulary Review   Vocabulary covered in this lesson is on page 281–287.

Who, What, When

Signers on video tell you which activity s/he did/will do on a particular day. Circle the day, write the activity, who and other information in the blanks. For purpose of this activity, "today" is Wednesday the 7th.

WHEN	WHO	WHAT

1.

S	M	T	W	T	F	S
				1	2	3
4	5	6	⑦	8	9	10
11	12	13	14	15	16	17
18	19	20	21	22	23	24
25	26	27	28	29	30	31

_____

Other information:

_____

2.

S	M	T	W	T	F	S
				1	2	3
4	5	6	⑦	8	9	10
11	12	13	14	15	16	17
18	19	20	21	22	23	24
25	26	27	28	29	30	31

_____

Other information:

_____

3.

S	M	T	W	T	F	S
				1	2	3
4	5	6	⑦	8	9	10
11	12	13	14	15	16	17
18	19	20	21	22	23	24
25	26	27	28	29	30	31

_____

Other information:

_____

4.

S	M	T	W	T	F	S
				1	2	3
4	5	6	⑦	8	9	10
11	12	13	14	15	16	17
18	19	20	21	22	23	24
25	26	27	28	29	30	31

_____

Other information:

_____

5.

S	M	T	W	T	F	S
				1	2	3
4	5	6	⑦	8	9	10
11	12	13	14	15	16	17
18	19	20	21	22	23	24
25	26	27	28	29	30	31

_____

Other information:

_____

6.

S	M	T	W	T	F	S
				1	2	3
4	5	6	⑦	8	9	10
11	12	13	14	15	16	17
18	19	20	21	22	23	24
25	26	27	28	29	30	31

_____

Other information:

_____

7.

S	M	T	W	T	F	S
				1	2	3
4	5	6	⑦	8	9	10
11	12	13	14	15	16	17
18	19	20	21	22	23	24
25	26	27	28	29	30	31

_____

Other information:

_____

8.

S	M	T	W	T	F	S
				1	2	3
4	5	6	⑦	8	9	10
11	12	13	14	15	16	17
18	19	20	21	22	23	24
25	26	27	28	29	30	31

_____

Other information:

_____

9.

S	M	T	W	T	F	S
				1	2	3
4	5	6	⑦	8	9	10
11	12	13	14	15	16	17
18	19	20	21	22	23	24
25	26	27	28	29	30	31

_____

Other information:

_____

10.

S	M	T	W	T	F	S
				1	2	3
4	5	6	(7)	8	9	10
11	12	13	14	15	16	17
18	19	20	21	22	23	24
25	26	27	28	29	30	31

_____

Other information:

_____

_____

11.

S	M	T	W	T	F	S
				1	2	3
4	5	6	(7)	8	9	10
11	12	13	14	15	16	17
18	19	20	21	22	23	24
25	26	27	28	29	30	31

_____

Other information:

_____

_____

12.

S	M	T	W	T	F	S
				1	2	3
4	5	6	(7)	8	9	10
11	12	13	14	15	16	17
18	19	20	21	22	23	24
25	26	27	28	29	30	31

_____

Other information:

_____

_____

13.

S	M	T	W	T	F	S
				1	2	3
4	5	6	(7)	8	9	10
11	12	13	14	15	16	17
18	19	20	21	22	23	24
25	26	27	28	29	30	31

_____

Other information:

_____

_____

Answers are given in class.

Homework 5:2

AGREEMENT VERBS

An agreement verb is a verb that indicates the subject (the person doing the action) and the object (the person receiving the action) in its movement. Usually the verb moves from the subject towards the object.

 View. In the following demonstrations, you will see a short skit on screen followed by each person retelling what happened from his/her point of view.

Show and Give

Observe how Ben, Michelle and Iva modify the movement of the verbs to describe these actions from their points of view. Note the movement of the verbs begins at the subject's location and ends at the object's location.

Ask and Tell

Observe how Isias, Norman and Priscilla modify the movement of the verbs to describe these actions from their points of view. Note the movement of the verbs begins at the subject's location and ends at the object's location.

Take and Throw

Observe how Tyrone, Melinda and Cinnie modify the movement of the verbs to describe these actions from their points of view. Note here the movement of the first verb is reversed, i.e., it begins at the location of the object and moves towards the subject.

Vocabulary Review   Vocabulary covered in this lesson is on pages 287–289.

Skits

You will see three more skits. After each skit, one of the actors retells two different versions of what happened. Put a check in the box below for the version that shows the correct verb agreement for all of the verbs.

Skit 1   A ☐   or   B ☐

Skit 2   A ☐   or   B ☐

Skit 3   A ☐   or   B ☐

Answers are given in class.

"Surprise for You"

Review the story on video. Observe how the movement of these verbs indicate the subject and object and agrees with the spatial location of the mother (which is up) and the child (which is down).

mother to child

child to mother

mother to child

New Signs

something that is unexpected; a surprise

to keep information from others; a secret

be unable to; can't

"G" AND "H" LETTERS

The hand positions for letters "G" and "H" can vary depending on what letter precedes or follows "G" or "H."

View. Cinnie demonstrates the basic hand positions for the letters "G" and "H."

"G" letter

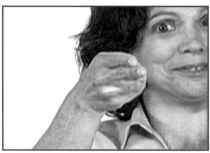
"H" letter

Now Cinnie will demonstrate the correct hand position for "G" and "H" in the following names.

Grace   Gayle   Doug
Holly   Hope   Philip

Practice fingerspelling the names. Pay attention to the position of the hand for the letters "G" and "H."

Write the Names

Melinda spells a list of names. Write the names below.

1. _____
2. _____
3. _____
4. _____
5. _____

6. _____
7. _____
8. _____
9. _____
10. _____

Answers are given in class.

Homework 5:4

 CONVERSATION 3

David (A) and Ben (B) demonstrate this dialogue in which Ben talks about chores among himself and his roommates. Observe where Ben designates locations for his roommates.

> Signers A & B: Discuss where B lives and what kind of residence
>
> B: Tell who (Khan and Sarah)
>
> A: Ask what each person's household chores are
>
> B: Name chores for each person (designate locations for each person)
>
> A: Ask if B doesn't mind doing his/her chore (specify chore)
>
> B: Give opinion
>
> A: Respond

DESIGNATING LOCATIONS FOR NON-PRESENT PEOPLE

In other units, you learned to discuss non-present people using strategies like contrastive structure or ranking on the non-dominant hand. Contrastive structure is only used to discuss two other people. Ranking is used to discuss items in a rank order such as a birth order.

But, if you want to talk about more than two non-present people, who are not in any rank order, you designate a location for each person along a horizontal arc in front of you starting on your non-dominant side.

When discussing each person,
- Be sure to orient signs toward the designated location when discussing that person, i.e. their chores
- Be sure the personal pronouns and possessive adjectives agree with the location when talking about the person

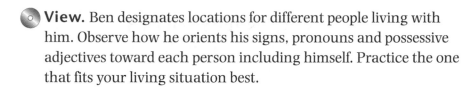**View.** Ben designates locations for different people living with him. Observe how he orients his signs, pronouns and possessive adjectives toward each person including himself. Practice the one that fits your living situation best.

One other person. Ben discusses his and Hannah's chores. Ben locates Hannah on his dominant side. Observe how he orients the possessive adjective and other signs towards the designated location while discussing Hannah's chores.

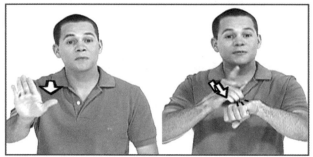

one other person Hannah designated on Ben's dominant side

refers to self

Two other people. Ben discusses his chores and those of two roommates. Observe how he designates the location for the first person in his non-dominant side, then the other roommate on his dominant side, and refers to himself last. Again, see where he orients his possessive adjectives and other signs.

first person Sage designated on Ben's non-dominant side

second person Henry designated on Ben's dominant side

refers to self

Three other people. Ben talks about the chores of three room-mates and his own. Observe how he designates the locations of the three people on an horizontal arc starting at his non-dominant side. Again, he orients his possessive adjectives and other signs accordingly.

first person Gloria designated on Ben's non-dominant side

second person Cheryl designated in front of Ben

third person Guy designated on Ben's dominant side

refers to self

MINIDIALOGUES

The three minidialogues show how locations are designated and possessive adjectives are used when talking about non-present people and their things. Write your answers below.

Minidialogue 1

1. Describe the three dogs and indicate who their owners are.

	description	owner
dog #1	_____ _____	_____
dog #2	_____ _____	_____
dog #3	_____ _____	_____

Minidialogue 2

1. Tell about the two cars Norman and his partner bought recently.

Norman's car: partner's car:

_____   _____

_____   _____

_____   _____

_____   _____

Minidialogue 3

1. Write down the information given about each of the four cups discussed.

	whose cup?	how did they get the cup?
cup #1	_____	_____
cup #2	_____	_____
cup #3	_____	_____
cup #4	_____	_____

Answers are given in class.

Vocabulary Review   Vocabulary covered in this lesson is on pages 289–293.

> **DID YOU REALIZE?**
> A Deaf baseball player named William Ellsworth Hoy brought hand signals to the major leagues in the late 1800's. When Hoy was at bat he had his third base coach use the hand signals to tell him the pitching count. It caught on with umpires and fans and to this day the same signals are used to call balls and strikes.

Homework 5:5

ARE YOU DONE?

To answer negatively to "Are you done....?" questions, use the sign below. For example, to answer the question "Are you done with vacuuming the floor?" you use the sign below to mean "No, I'm not done yet."

negative response

To respond affirmatively to the same question, use the sign below to mean "Yes, I'm done."

affirmative response

View. Michelle asks "Are you done...?" followed by Isias demonstrating two different responses – one negative and the other affirmative.

⊙ MINIDIALOGUES

Watch the four dialogues and answer the questions below.

Minidialogue 1

1. What does Norman ask Melinda?

2. What do Norman and Melinda agree to do?

Minidialogue 2

1. Why does Iva point out the man with the green shirt?

2. What are Iva and Priscilla going to do?

Minidialogue 3

1. What does Ben ask David about?

2. What does Ben ask David to do?

3. What does David suggest?

Minidialogue 4

1. What does Joey ask Cinnie about?

2. What does Joey offer to do for Cinnie?

3. Why does Cinnie decline the offer?

4. When are the books due?

Answers are given in class.

Homework 5:6

CONVERSATION 4

Iva (A) and Stefanie (B) demonstrate this dialogue in which Stefanie discusses two errands she needs to do.

> **Signers A & B:** Greet, then discuss B's dog and where it goes to get groomed
> **A:** Invite B to join her
> **B:** Decline, tell about two errands; suggest another day
> **A:** Respond, suggest different day
> **B:** Give opinion
> **A & B:** close the conversation

Key Grammar

SEQUENCING ACTIVITIES

One way to talk about activities you did or will do on a certain day is to designate a location in your signing space for each of the activities. Begin by establishing the first activity on your non-dominant side, then your final activity on your dominant side.

To sequence two activities, do the following:

1. use different locations in your signing space to represent each activity and orient signs about the activity toward that space.
2. use the sign at left to transition from one activity to the next transition sign
3. make sure the movement of the verb for "to go" shows agreement with the activities' established locations.
4. raise your brows and head at the beginning of the "transition" sign
5. lower your head at the end of the sign

transition sign

Sequencing Activities

Stefanie demonstrates sequencing two activities from Conversation 4. Pay attention to the non-manual behaviors that accompany the transition sign.

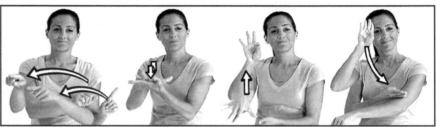

Sign Tip

When you say you are going somewhere, for example, "I'm going to the doctor," or "I'm going to the gas station," you can use either sign (below) to make the statement.

act of leaving to do something

act of going to a specific place to do something

However, if you are talking about doing two or more activities; i.e., sequencing activities, you can *only* use the sign above on the right.

First and Second

Ben and Iva sequence two activities each. See how the answers are marked below the pictures corresponding with the activities in the example on the next page, Ben 1, Ben 2, Iva 1, and Iva 2.

Watch the rest of the sentences. Below the pictures of the activities, write the name of the signer and 1 or 2 to indicate the sequence.

Example

Ben 2 _____ | Iva 2 _____ | Iva 1 _____ | Ben 1 _____

1.

_____ _____ _____ _____

2.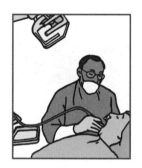

_____ _____ _____ _____

3.

_____ _____ _____ _____

4.

_____   _____   _____   _____

5.

_____   _____   _____   _____

6.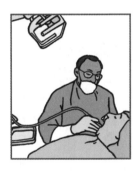

_____   _____   _____   _____

7.

_____   _____   _____   _____

8.

_____ _____ _____ _____

9.

_____ _____ _____ _____

Answers are given in class.

🔘 TRANSLATING ENGLISH QUESTIONS WITH "DO"

Here are five tips to translate English sentences with "do" into ASL.

Translation Tip 1

To translate questions with "What did you do…?, "What will you be doing…?," or "What should I do?," use the sign at left.

Watch how David translates "What did your brother do yesterday?"

Wh-word question asking what one did/ will do

Translation Tip 2

Use this sign phrase to ask what a person "needs to do," "is required to do," or "is expected to do."

Watch how David translates "What does your father need to do tomorrow?

Translation Tip 3

To translate questions with "Did you...?" "Have you...?" or "Are you done with...?" use the sign at left.

Watch how David translates "Did you clean the house?"

Translation Tip 4

If you want to ask questions that begin with "Do you...?, translate them by using raised brows in a yes-no question.

Watch how David translates "Do you like candy?" Notice that "do" is incorporated in the non-manual markers for the yes-no question.

Translation Tip 5

For English phrases like "doing laundry," or "doing homework," change the noun "laundry" or "homework" to verbs like "washing clothes" or "writing homework."

Watch how David translates "When will you do the laundry?"
Notice that "do" is incorporated in the sign for "washing clothes."

Activity

Read each sentence below and determine which of the tips you would use to translate the sentence into ASL. Mark with the number for the tip.

_____**1.** Do you like his new motorcycle?   _____**6.** What are you doing Sunday?

_____**2.** Did you see the movie?   _____**7.** What will your mother do on her birthday?

_____**3.** Do you know her?   _____**8.** What did the doctor tell you to do?

_____**4.** What do you need to do tomorrow?   _____**9.** Did you do your homework?

_____**5.** How do you do that?   _____**10.** When will you do the dishes?

Now, try and translate all of the sentences.

Answers are given in class.

Vocabulary Review   Vocabulary covered in this lesson is on pages 293–298.

Homework 5:7

TELL HOW OFTEN

When discussing how often one does an activity, use the following phrases to indicate the level of frequency.

Calendar A

S	M	T	W	T	F	S
				1	2	3
4	5	6	7	8	9	10
11	12	13	14	15	16	17
18	19	20	21	22	23	24
25	26	27	28	29	30	31

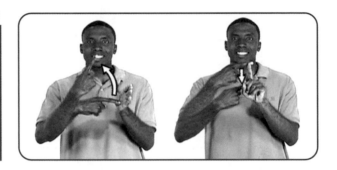

Calendar B

S	M	T	W	T	F	S
				1	2	3
4	5	6	7	8	9	10
11	12	13	14	15	16	17
18	19	20	21	22	23	24
25	26	27	28	29	30	31

Calendar C

S	M	T	W	T	F	S
				1	2	3
4	5	6	7	8	9	10
11	12	13	14	15	16	17
18	19	20	21	22	23	24
25	26	27	28	29	30	31

Calendar D

S	M	T	W	T	F	S
				1	2	3
4	5	6	7	8	9	10
11	12	13	14	15	16	17
18	19	20	21	22	23	24
25	26	27	28	29	30	31

Calendar E

S	M	T	W	T	F	S
				1	2	3
4	5	6	7	8	9	10
11	12	13	14	15	16	17
18	19	20	21	22	23	24
25	26	27	28	29	30	31

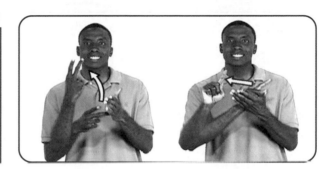

Calendar F

S	M	T	W	T	F	S
				1	2	3
4	5	6	7	8	9	10
11	12	13	14	15	16	17
18	19	20	21	22	23	24
25	26	27	28	29	30	31

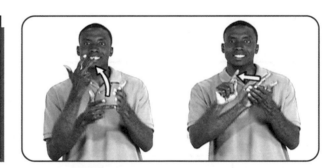

Calendar G

S	M	T	W	T	F	S
				1	2	3
4	5	6	7	8	9	10
11	12	13	14	15	16	17
18	19	20	21	22	23	24
25	26	27	28	29	30	31

Calendar H

S	M	T	W	T	F	S
				1	2	3
4	5	6	7	8	9	10
11	12	13	14	15	16	17
18	19	20	21	22	23	24
25	26	27	28	29	30	31

Sign Tip When asking someone "how often" he or she does an activity, use this yes-no question.

ask how often a person goes to the library to study

Who Did What How Often?

Priscilla and Isias discuss how often a person does a particular activity. Write down the name and activity, then circle the letter that corresponds to the calendar that correctly shows how often (see calendars on pages 258–259).

who	activity	Calendar (how often)
1.		A B C D E F G H
2.		A B C D E F G H
3.		A B C D E F G H
4.		A B C D E F G H
5.		A B C D E F G H
6.		A B C D E F G H
7.		A B C D E F G H
8.		A B C D E F G H

Answers are given in class.

Vocabulary Review Vocabulary for this lesson is on pages 299–300.

Homework 5:8

⊙ CONVERSATION 5

Joey (A) and Tyrone (B) demonstrate this dialogue in which Tyrone tells about an "out of the ordinary" activity he did.

> **Signers A & B:** Greet each other
>
> **A:** Mention he hasn't seen B in a while, ask what B has been doing
>
> **B:** Describe basic routine, then talk about one "out of the ordinary" activity (Oakland Art Festival)
> - when
> - with who
> - did what
> - comment on the activity
>
> **A:** Respond and ask follow up questions

Key 🔑 Grammar

TELL ABOUT AN "OUT OF THE ORDINARY" ACTIVITY

When someone asks you what's been happening to you, you can give a brief description of your ordinary routine and then elaborate on an activity that is "out of the ordinary," something in your recent schedule that was pleasurable or unusual.

To do this, you need to:

Begin with this transition sign to signal you are going to talk about an out of the ordinary activity. Note that this sign differs from the cardinal number 1 in how it is expressed.

transition sign

Elaborate on the activity by following this sequence:

1. tell what happened

2. tell who you did the activity with, using a plural pronoun if needed

3. tell what you did, giving adequate details so your listener can appreciate your out of the ordinary experience

4. end the description by commenting on your experience

⊙ *Out of the Ordinary*

Tyrone demonstrates how to describe an out of the ordinary activity he and his brother recently did from Conversation 5. Notice how he follows the sequence:

1. Tell when (day, part of day)

Tyrone establishes the tense with a time sign phrase (last week, Sunday afternoon).

2. Tell with who (plural pronouns)

Tyrone then mentions who the other person was and uses plural pronoun to indicate he and his brother did the activity together. Notice he doesn't say "me" because this plural pronoun refers to both Tyrone and his brother.

3. Tell what you did

Tyrone now names the "out of the ordinary" activity which was going to the Oakland Arts Festival. Observe how he adds details such as walking, sightseeing, eating, shopping, and buying a beautiful painting.

4. Comment on the activity

Finally, Tyrone ends his description expressing how much he enjoyed the activity.

PLURAL PRONOUNS

Plural pronouns indicate that a number of people did something together. To use those plural pronouns, do the following:

• name the other people i.e. "my friend", "my sister", "my parents", "my children"

• use the corresponding plural pronoun to represent them and yourself. There is no need to say "I/me." The plural pronoun properly used implies you are among them. Here are some examples:

One other person and yourself

To refer to the other person and yourself, reverse your upright 'K' hand and toggle the hand back and forth repeatedly between "the other person" (usually located on your dominant side) and yourself.

"the two of us..."

Two to four other people and yourself

To refer to two to four other people and yourself, tilt your "3," "4," or "5" hand forward and move it in a circular motion (reverse it, if you are left-handed). Be sure the last finger of your hand is oriented toward you to indicate you are part of the group e.g., the middle finger of the "3" hand, or the pinky finger of the "4" and "5" hands.

"the three of us..."   **"the four of us..."**   **"the five of us..."**

For more than five other people and yourself

To refer to over five people and yourself, point your index finger down, start on the dominant side of your chest, and trace an arc in front of your body towards the other side of the chest.

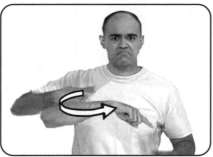

"all of us..."

TIME CONCEPTS—BEYOND THE CURRENT WEEK

In this unit you learned to refer to six days preceding yesterday using this sign plus the sign for the day. For this, "today" is Wednesday the 18th.

S	M	T	W	T	F	S
1	2	3	4	5	6	7
8	9	10	11	12	13	14
15	16	17	(18)	19	20	21
22	23	24	25	26	27	28
29	30	31				

For example, to refer to Monday the 16th, use the sign phrase below:

You also learned to refer to six days following tomorrow by using this sign plus the sign for the day.

For example, to refer to Monday the 23rd, use the sign phrase below:

If you want to refer to the whole week of the 8th through 14th, use this sign alone.

If you said you went to a baseball game on Monday the 9th, add the sign for "Monday" to the sign above:

S	M	T	W	T	F	S
1	2	3	4	5	6	7
8	9	10	11	12	13	14
15	16	17	18	19	20	21
22	23	24	25	26	27	28
29	30	31				

Do the same for the 8th and 10th.

To refer to the whole week of the 22nd through the 28th, use the sign below plus the sign for the day.

S	M	T	W	T	F	S
1	2	3	4	5	6	7
8	9	10	11	12	13	14
15	16	17	18	19	20	21
22	23	24	25	26	27	28
29	30	31				

If you said you plan to go see a movie on Friday the 27th, you would add the sign for "Friday" to the above sign:

S	M	T	W	T	F	S
1	2	3	4	5	6	7
8	9	10	11	12	13	14
15	16	17	18	19	20	21
22	23	24	25	26	27	28
29	30	31				

Do the same for the 26th and 28th.

⊙ Circle the Day, Part of the Day

Watch Norman give time phrases. Circle the day of the week, and the part of the day indicated. For the purpose of this activity, "today" is Wednesday the 14th.

1. DAY

S	M	T	W	T	F	S
4	5	6	7	8	9	10
11	12	13	(14)	15	16	17
18	19	20	21	22	23	24

PART OF DAY: AM PM EVE

2. DAY

S	M	T	W	T	F	S
4	5	6	7	8	9	10
11	12	13	(14)	15	16	17
18	19	20	21	22	23	24

PART OF DAY: AM PM EVE

3. DAY

S	M	T	W	T	F	S
4	5	6	7	8	9	10
11	12	13	(14)	15	16	17
18	19	20	21	22	23	24

PART OF DAY: AM PM EVE

4. DAY

S	M	T	W	T	F	S
4	5	6	7	8	9	10
11	12	13	(14)	15	16	17
18	19	20	21	22	23	24

PART OF DAY: AM PM EVE

5. DAY

S	M	T	W	T	F	S
4	5	6	7	8	9	10
11	12	13	(14)	15	16	17
18	19	20	21	22	23	24

PART OF DAY: AM PM EVE

6. DAY

S	M	T	W	T	F	S
4	5	6	7	8	9	10
11	12	13	(14)	15	16	17
18	19	20	21	22	23	24

PART OF DAY: AM PM EVE

7. DAY

S	M	T	W	T	F	S
4	5	6	7	8	9	10
11	12	13	(14)	15	16	17
18	19	20	21	22	23	24

PART OF DAY: AM PM EVE

8. DAY

S	M	T	W	T	F	S
4	5	6	7	8	9	10
11	12	13	(14)	15	16	17
18	19	20	21	22	23	24

PART OF DAY: AM PM EVE

9. DAY

S	M	T	W	T	F	S
4	5	6	7	8	9	10
11	12	13	(14)	15	16	17
18	19	20	21	22	23	24

PART OF DAY: AM PM EVE

10. DAY

S	M	T	W	T	F	S
4	5	6	7	8	9	10
11	12	13	(14)	15	16	17
18	19	20	21	22	23	24

PART OF DAY: AM PM EVE

11. DAY

S	M	T	W	T	F	S
4	5	6	7	8	9	10
11	12	13	(14)	15	16	17
18	19	20	21	22	23	24

PART OF DAY: AM PM EVE

12. DAY

S	M	T	W	T	F	S
4	5	6	7	8	9	10
11	12	13	(14)	15	16	17
18	19	20	21	22	23	24

PART OF DAY: AM PM EVE

Answers on page 417.

◉ *Tell about Activities*

Signers tell which activity they will do/did on a particular day. Circle the day and part of the day, tell who, and what activity was mentioned. For purpose of this activity, "today" is Wednesday the 14th.

1.   **WHEN**   **WHO**   **DESCRIBE ACTIVITY**

S	M	T	W	T	F	S
4	5	6	7	8	9	10
11	12	13	(14)	15	16	17
18	19	20	21	22	23	24

_____   _____

Other information given:

PART OF DAY: AM PM EVE

_____

_____

2.   **WHEN**   **WHO**   **DESCRIBE ACTIVITY**

S	M	T	W	T	F	S
4	5	6	7	8	9	10
11	12	13	(14)	15	16	17
18	19	20	21	22	23	24

_____   _____

Other information given:

PART OF DAY: AM PM EVE

_____

_____

3.   **WHEN**   **WHO**   **DESCRIBE ACTIVITY**

S	M	T	W	T	F	S
4	5	6	7	8	9	10
11	12	13	(14)	15	16	17
18	19	20	21	22	23	24

_____   _____

Other information given:

PART OF DAY: AM PM EVE

_____

4.   **WHEN**   **WHO**   **DESCRIBE ACTIVITY**

S	M	T	W	T	F	S
4	5	6	7	8	9	10
11	12	13	(14)	15	16	17
18	19	20	21	22	23	24

_____   _____

Other information given:

PART OF DAY: AM PM EVE

_____

5.   **WHEN**

S	M	T	W	T	F	S
4	5	6	7	8	9	10
11	12	13	(14)	15	16	17
18	19	20	21	22	23	24

PART OF DAY: AM   PM   EVE

WHO

_____

Other information given:

_____

DESCRIBE ACTIVITY

_____

_____

_____

---

6.   **WHEN**

S	M	T	W	T	F	S
4	5	6	7	8	9	10
11	12	13	(14)	15	16	17
18	19	20	21	22	23	24

PART OF DAY: AM   PM   EVE

WHO

_____

Other information given:

_____

DESCRIBE ACTIVITY

_____

_____

_____

---

7.   **WHEN**

S	M	T	W	T	F	S
4	5	6	7	8	9	10
11	12	13	(14)	15	16	17
18	19	20	21	22	23	24

PART OF DAY: AM   PM   EVE

WHO

_____

Other information given:

_____

DESCRIBE ACTIVITY

_____

_____

_____

---

8.   **WHEN**

S	M	T	W	T	F	S
4	5	6	7	8	9	10
11	12	13	(14)	15	16	17
18	19	20	21	22	23	24

PART OF DAY: AM   PM   EVE

WHO

_____

Other information given:

_____

DESCRIBE ACTIVITY

_____

_____

_____

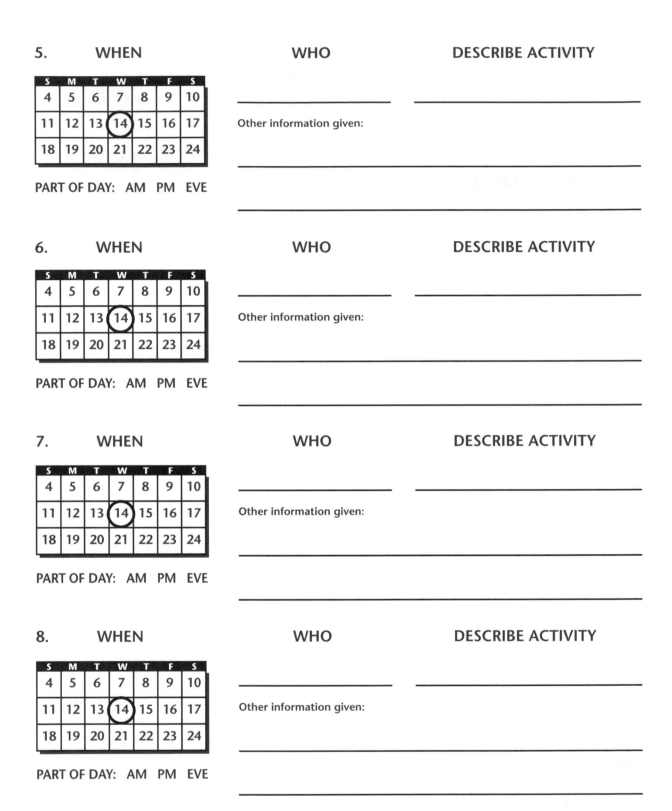

9.   **WHEN**

S	M	T	W	T	F	S
4	5	6	7	8	9	10
11	12	13	(14)	15	16	17
18	19	20	21	22	23	24

PART OF DAY: AM PM EVE

WHO

_____

Other information given:

DESCRIBE ACTIVITY

_____

_____

_____

10.   **WHEN**

S	M	T	W	T	F	S
4	5	6	7	8	9	10
11	12	13	(14)	15	16	17
18	19	20	21	22	23	24

PART OF DAY: AM PM EVE

WHO

_____

Other information given:

DESCRIBE ACTIVITY

_____

_____

_____

Answers are given in class.

Test Yourself

Using this calendar, answer the following questions. For purpose of this activity, today's date is the 16th.

S	M	T	W	T	F	S
1	2	3	4	5	6	7
8	9	10	11	12	13	14
15	(16)	17	18	19	20	21
22	23	24	25	26	27	28
29	30	31				

Which days on the calendar can be referred to using the sign below? List the dates.

1.

_____

2.

_____

3.

_____

4.

_____

Answers on page 418.

Vocabulary Review   Vocabulary for this lesson is on pages 301–306.

Homework 5:9

COMMONLY FINGERSPELLED WORDS

Congratulations! You have learned and practiced how to form all letters in the manual alphabet. So far, you have learned to finger-spell mostly proper nouns, i.e., names of people and places. While it is possible to fingerspell every English word, it is just not done! Only certain words have been "borrowed" from English and used commonly in ASL as "signs." For example here are two categories where commonly fingerspelled words are found:

- short, easy to fingerspell, words (mostly nouns)
- specific kinds in a group, e.g.
   - types of bread (wheat, rye),
   - kinds of housing (duplex, flat, ranch),
   - types of material (nylon, cotton, polyester)

With the following exercises, you learn and practice some of the commonly fingerspelled words. Again, do not be tempted to finger-spell just any English word. Remember if you don't know or forgot the sign, use the techniques learned earlier to ask for it.

Sign Tip

Understanding Fingerspelling

1. watch the movement of the letters to help figure out the fingerspelled word

2. use context provided by the sentence to help understand what word is spelled

3. catch the first few letters and last letter and relying on context, make an educated guess for the word

Write the Word 1

Signers give sentences containing the commonly fingerspelled words from the list below. Write down the fingerspelled word.

PRIZE	PUPPY	SIZE
BILLS	JUNK	TEE
VEST	BAG	GIFT
COUCH	X-RAY*	QUILT

1._____   5._____   9._____

2._____   6._____   10._____

3._____   7._____   11._____

4._____   8._____   12._____

Answers on page 418.

Word List 1

Now Cinnie demonstrates how to fingerspell the words above.

Challenge Yourself   In a day or two, get a separate sheet of paper, replay the "Word List 1" segment and write down the words Cinnie fingersspells. Replay this segment until you can recognize the word as much by the movement as by the letters spelled.

---

*In "X-ray," the letter "x" is made in a circular movement. Any letter that stands alone uses a circular movement, except for J and Z.

Write the Word 2

Signers present more sentences that contain other commonly fingerspelled words from the list below. Write the fingerspelled word only.

VAN	TV	HERB	TWIN
ICE	BBQ	DESK	JUICE
ZOO	FAX	CONDO	PLASTIC
GAS	HAM	TRUCK	BURRITO

1._____ 5._____ 9._____ 13._____

2._____ 6._____ 10._____ 14._____

3._____ 7._____ 11._____ 15._____

4._____ 8._____ 12._____ 16._____

Answers on page 419.

Word List 2

Cinnie demonstrates how to fingerspell the words listed above.

Challenge Yourself   In a day or two, get another sheet of paper, replay the "Word List 2" segment and write down the word fingerspelled in the sentences.

DID YOU REALIZE?
That signing villages once existed in America? For more than 100 years in certain villages on Martha's Vineyard, an island off Cape Cod, as many as 1 out of 25 people were Deaf (compared to 1 in 6000 on the mainland) and all the inhabitants, Deaf or hearing, used Sign Language.

CLAYTON VALLI (1951-2003)

Clayton Valli used his natural gift for eloquent ASL, his curiosity and drive, to study his language and make a lasting contribution to ASL Poetry and Linguistics.

Valli was born in Massachusetts and attended the Austine School for the Deaf in Vermont. He received a Bachelor's from the University of Nevada, Reno, in 1978, a Master's in linguistics from Gallaudet University in 1985, and received a Ph.D. in ASL Poetry from the Union Institute in Ohio in 1993. His Ph.D. was a personal triumph, but was also a quantum leap in the field of ASL poetics. Many researchers had included ASL poetry in their broader study of ASL, but Valli deepened and expanded this research.

He studied rhyme, rhythm, and meter found in ASL poetry, and discussed common motifs, alliteration, and repetition, becoming a motivating force in the recognition of ASL poetry as a genre of literature in its own right.

Valli recalled the first time he was inspired by the creativity of ASL when what he thought was an insult from a young Deaf boy was really a number poem in ASL. Valli was fascinated by this creation and wanted to make his own poems in ASL. At the time the recognition and acceptance of ASL as a complete language was relatively new, although Valli already believed in ASL as a beautiful boundless language that could express anything.

Valli became engrossed in the patterns and features of poetic ASL, seeing that they paralleled features studied in traditional written poetics. He studied rhyme, rhythm, and meter found in ASL poetry, and discussed common motifs, alliteration, and repetition, becoming a motivating force in the recognition of ASL poetry as a genre of literature in its own right.

His poetry is revered in the Deaf community, and some of his best work combines his experience of the beauty of the world and his language. At the same time Valli did not shy away from difficult themes of language oppression, and being misunderstood in a world that was not always friendly. Some of his best-known works are "Dandelion," "Snowflake," and "Lone Sturdy Tree." His poetry is captured on the videotape *Poetry in Motion*, and the DVD *ASL Poetry: Selected Works of Clayton Valli*. It was always Valli's strong belief that ASL Poetry was something for all to create and enjoy, and his work still impacts ASL poets.

Valli taught at Gallaudet University, and co-authored many books on ASL including *Linguistics of American Sign Language, Language Contact in the Deaf Community, What's Your Sign for Pizza*, and served as editor-in-chief for *The Gallaudet Dictionary of American Sign Language*.

Valli was a pioneer in researching and raising awareness of ASL poetry. He passed away in 2003, but generations of ASL poets and researchers will benefit from his dedication to, love for, and unique expression of ASL.

QUESTIONS TO ASK

Now that you have reached the end of Unit 5, you should be able to ask the following questions. Read the cue for each question, think about how you would ask it, and watch Melinda sign the question. Then find a partner and practice signing the questions (and answers) to each other.

1. ask what the person did last Saturday.

2. ask when the person does laundry.

3. ask if the person exercises everyday.

4. ask what errands the person must do tomorrow.

5. ask the person who s/he lives with and what their household duties are.

6. ask the person if s/he minds washing dishes.

7. explain you have not finished your homework, ask the person if s/he has done his/her homework.

8. explain you must go to the post office to mail a package, then to the bank to get some money. Ask the person if s/he wants to come with you.

9. explain you and your roommate are moving to another apartment next Friday. Ask the person if s/he can help you move.

10. explain you and two friends are going to the museum this afternoon. Ask the person to join you.

AUTOBIOGRAPHIES

Cinnie, Tyrone, and Stefanie add to Emma's, Billy's, and Sara's autobiographies. Summarize the information given.

Autobiography 1

Name __Emma__
Summarize information:

_____

_____

_____

_____

Autobiography 2

Name __Billy__
Summarize information:

_____

_____

_____

_____

Autobiography 3

Name __Sarah__
Summarize information:

_____

_____

_____

_____

Answers on pages 419–420.

SELF-ASSESSMENT

Now that you are done with this unit, rate yourself using the list below: 5 indicates feeling the most comfortable and confident about your skill in that area and 1 indicates feeling the least confident.

NOTE: If you marked 3 or below on any skill area, you should review that portion of the workbook.

1. I am able to ask what someone did/will do on a certain day.	5	4	3	2	1
2. I am able to ask when someone did/will do a certain activity.	5	4	3	2	1
3. I am able to ask someone if s/he has completed an activity.	5	4	3	2	1
4. I am able to ask and tell someone how often one does an activity.	5	4	3	2	1
5. I know how to use time signs to discuss events in the future and in the past.	5	4	3	2	1
6. I know how to express opinions.	5	4	3	2	1
7. I know how to use space around me when using possessive adjectives to discuss more than 2 people.	5	4	3	2	1
8. I know how to use agreement verbs to indicate the subject and the object of an action.	5	4	3	2	1
9. I know how and when to indicate tense in a sentence.	5	4	3	2	1
10. I know how to use non-manual markers to sequence two or more activities.	5	4	3	2	1
11. I know the correct forms for plural pronouns to tell how many.	5	4	3	2	1
12. I know the correct sign to use when responding to a "Are you done…?" question.	5	4	3	2	1
13. I am able to correctly fingerspell the letters "G" and "H."	5	4	3	2	1
14. I know the vocabulary used in this unit.	5	4	3	2	1

Wh-Word Question Signs

ask when

or

ask what person did/will do

Time Signs

the present day

the day before today

or

the day after today

in the general past

in the future

or

S	M	T	W	T	F	S
1	2	3	4	5	6	7

S	M	T	W	T	F	S
1	2	3	4	5	6	7

S	M	T	W	T	F	S
1	2	3	4	5	6	7

S	M	T	W	T	F	S
1	2	3	4	5	6	7

or

S	M	T	W	T	F	S
1	2	3	4	5	6	7

S	M	T	W	T	F	S
1	2	3	4	5	6	7

S	M	T	W	T	F	S
1	2	3	4	5	6	7

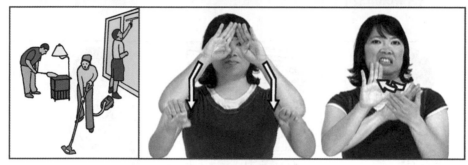

to go to a place

**to go do something;
to leave for a place**

Places

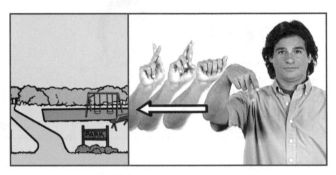

Category Sign

Show and Give

me to you

you to me

she/he to her/him

me to you

you to me

she/he to her/him

Ask and Tell

me to you

you to me

she/he to her/him

me to you

you to me

she/he to her/him

Take and Throw

me from you

you from me

she/he to her/him

me to you

you to me

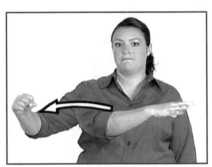

she/he to her/him

me to you

you to me

she/he to her/him

Object

Chores

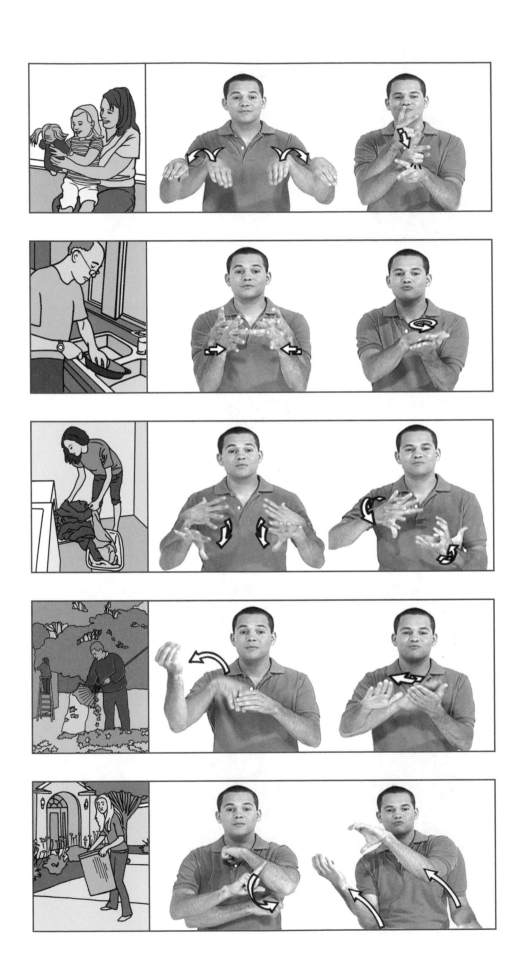

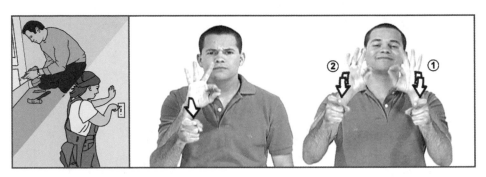

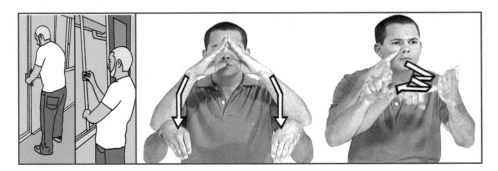

Category Sign

**task(s) or chore(s)
a person is expected
to perform**

Opinions about Chores

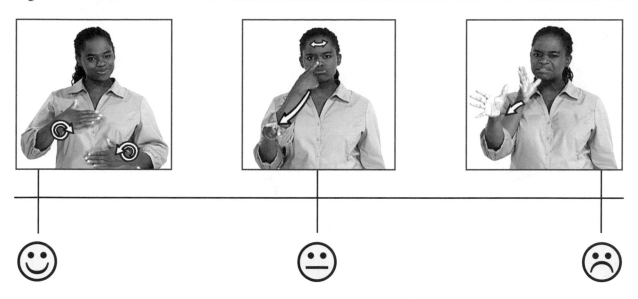

😊   😐   ☹

Ask if Done: Responses

not completed yet   completed

Errands

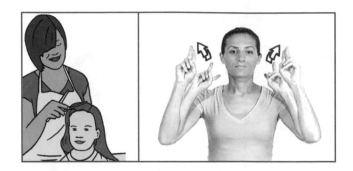

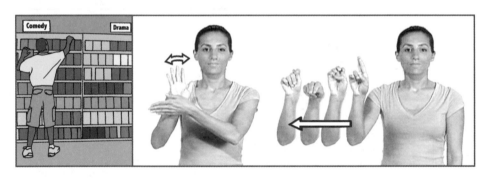

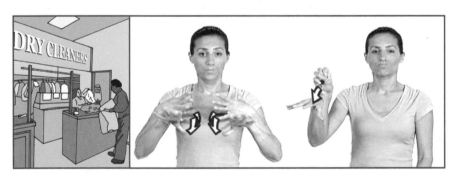

OIL CHANGE

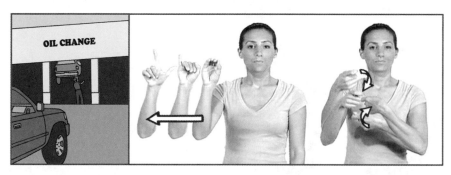

Places

or

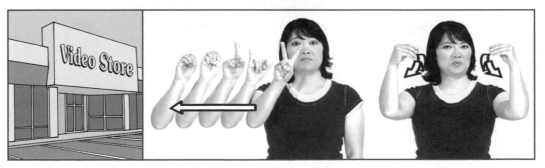

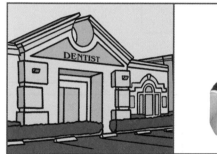  or

 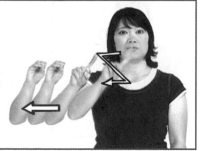

Transition Sign

and then; after that; and next

Wh-Word Question

ask what one needs to do

Levels of Willingness

willing

not willing

Responses

acknowledge information

express amazement

express sympathy

S	M	T	W	T	F	S
1	2	3	4	5	6	7
8	9	10	11	12	13	14
15	16	17	18	19	20	21
22	23	24	25	26	27	28
29	30	31				

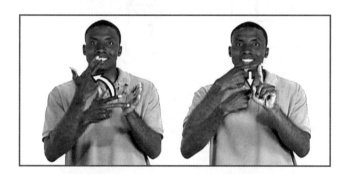

S	M	T	W	T	F	S
1	2	3	4	5	6	7
8	9	10	11	12	13	14
15	16	17	18	19	20	21
22	23	24	25	26	27	28
29	30	31				

S	M	T	W	T	F	S
1	2	3	4	5	6	7
8	9	10	11	12	13	14
15	16	17	18	19	20	21
22	23	24	25	26	27	28
29	30	31				

S	M	T	W	T	F	S
1	2	3	4	5	6	7

S	M	T	W	T	F	S
1	2	3	4	5	6	7

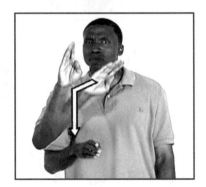

Time Signs

the week after this week

the week before this week

Parts of Day

all day long

Plural Pronouns

two of us

three of us

four of us

five of us

all of us

Activities with Others

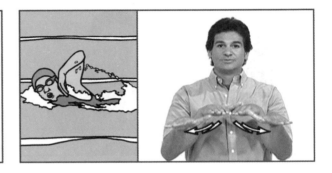

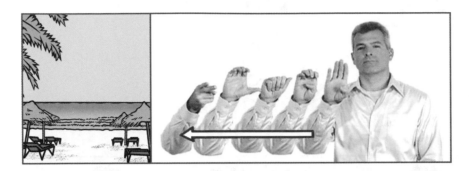

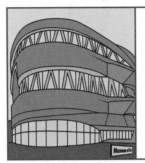   

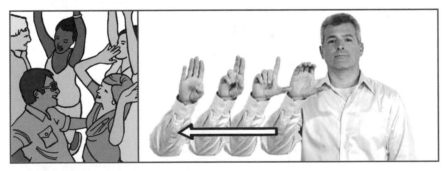

Comments on Activities

a good time; lots of fun

pleasant, delightful, nice

to get pleasure from

Other Signs

since the last time

remaining the same;
no changes

Transition Sign

used to signal a person
is about to talk about
something out of the
ordinary

Invite

**be obligated to;
be required to**

ask to participate

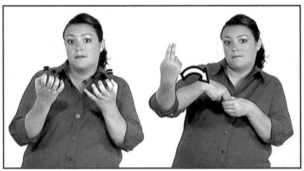

ask to take part in an activity

ask to assist someone

Respond to Invitation

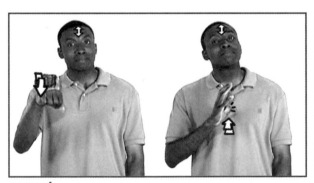

accept

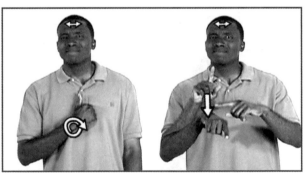

decline

Storytelling

UNIT 6

Storytelling

Homework 6:1

💿 TIMBER

"Timber" is a well-known folktale told within the Deaf community. Joey tells the story of a lumberjack who realizes that a tree is "deaf" and that yelling "timber" won't bring that tree down.

NEW VOCABULARY

to let one know, inform, to tell, to give an account of

narration, tale, story

to work, to have a job; occupation, place of work

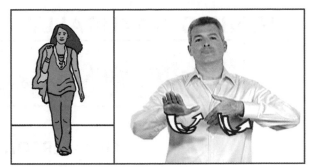

in that area (or location)   to be starved or hungry

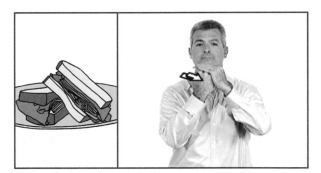

ONE-PERSON ROLE SHIFT IN NARRATIVES

Focus: Practice one-person role shift to show how a character behaved.

One-person role shift allows the narrator to show how a character behaves. The narrator becomes the character, taking on his/her actions, manners and feelings. For example, in this story, the narrator shifts to the lumberjack to show him looking over a tree, picking up the ax and chopping the tree down. Effective role shift involves both your body and your eyes. Your eye gaze must appear as if you are "truly" looking at the person, place or thing you are interacting with or referring to. All these elements must be in agreement for the role shift to be successful.

 View. The following scenes in the story use one-person role shift:

Lumberjack Walking

Joey becomes the lumberjack and walks, holding his ax over his right shoulder and lunch pail in his left hand, looking around at the environment.

Looking at First Tree

Joey becomes the lumberjack and looks upwards to gauge how tall (and how big) the tree is. For each successive tree, adjust your eye gaze and exaggerate the description of the tree to indicate the next tree is bigger and taller.

Chopping Down the Tree

Joey becomes the lumberjack and chops the tree. Then he shows how the ax hits the tree trunk using the "B" handshape and the tree starting to fall.

NOTE: As you transition from showing the lumberjack gripping and swinging the ax to using the "B" handshape to show where the ax struck the trunk, make sure both motions come from the same side, like Joey does, swinging right to left.

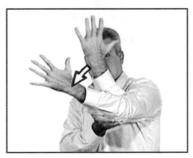

Yelling "Timber"

Joey becomes the lumberjack, cupping his hands around his mouth and then mouthing the word "Timber" as if yelling. Eye gaze should be directed up at the imaginary tree in front of the signer.

NOTE: The signer raises his brows when he names the objects – coffee, sandwich and apple. Practice the scene again and raise your brows when you name the object.

Eating Lunch

Joey becomes the lumberjack and opens his lunch pail, taking out and drinking his coffee; taking out and eating his sandwich; taking out, eating and disposing of his apple; putting away his thermos and gathering up his things (ax and lunch pail).

Homework 6:3

TWO-PERSON ROLE SHIFT IN NARRATIVES

Focus: Practice two-person role shift to show the interaction between the lumberjack and the doctor.

Two-person role shift allows the narrator to show interactions between two characters in a story. The narrator shifts between the two characters, adopting each character's actions, manners, and feelings as well as comments.

In the story "Timber," Joey uses two-person role shift to show the conversation between the lumberjack and the doctor. First, he establishes the doctor to the left of the lumberjack. Then consistently shifts to assume these locations and characters to continue the story.

as the doctor

as the lumberjack

To role shift, turn your head just enough to complete the shift but not so much that the listener cannot see your facial expressions. Only your upper body and head turn slightly to make the shift. Do not move your feet.

View. The following scene uses two-person role shift:

NOTE: Be sure when you show the doctor putting the stethoscope to his ears to listen to the tree, that the placement of the stethoscope agrees spatially with where the tree has been established (slightly to the doctor's right).

The Lumberjack and the Doctor

Using Joey's point of view, the doctor enters the scene from the **left.** Joey orients his upper body so it is consistent with the placement of the doctor and looks **to the right side** (at the lumberjack) when signing the doctor's lines. Likewise, when it is the lumberjack's turn to speak, Joey looks to the left (at the doctor) when signing the lumberjack's lines.

Homework 6:4

STORY COHESION

Focus: Practice elements needed to tell a story well.

• transitions (raised brows)

• engaging the audience

• use of signing space

• the ending

Transitions

Use *raised brows* to signal the beginning of a new scene or segment.

View. A number will appear on screen to point out when Joey uses the transition (listed below). Practice raising your brows to introduce each scene.

1.

introduces the
lumberjack

2.

lumberjack going to work

3.

introduces the forest

For the following three transitions (4-6), Joey begins by role shifting the lumberjack looking upward at the tree, then putting his ax and lunch pail down before raising his brows and giving the sign for the "tree."

4.

introduces the 1st tree

5.

introduces the 2nd tree

6.

introduces the last tree

7.

physician arriving at the scene

Engaging the Audience

To tell the story well, you must engage your audience. One way to do this is to make deliberate eye contact with your audience and maintain the eye contact throughout the story. With eye contact, the listener is more attentive to the story. The only time you should break eye contact with the audience is when you role shift to a character. If you are to tell the story to a camera, imagine the camera is your audience and remember the only time you can look away from the camera is when you are using role shift.

Another important way to engage your audience is to tell the story with deliberate enthusiasm. The only way to do this is to step into the story and make it come alive.

Use of Signing Space

To make the presentation visually appealing, work on making your signs larger and deliberate.

The Ending

To tell this humorous story well, practice the ending by...

- spelling the word "timber" in a dramatic fashion

- showing the tree landing hard on the ground

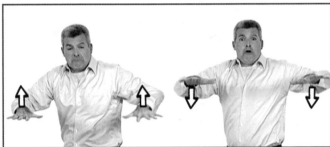

- concluding with the "thumbs up" exchange between the lumberjack and the physician, and toward the listener/audience at the end of the story.

Day of Filming

On the day of the filming, please adhere to the following:

- Wear solid color clothes.
- If your hair tends to fall into your eyes, pin it back or wear a ponytail.
- Don't wear hats (unless it has no brim) because of the shadows hiding your face.
- You should have nothing in your mouth – no candy or gum while filming. If you have something in your mouth you run the risk of not executing the "face grammar" correctly, possibly resulting in a lower grade.

Homework 6:5

💿 THE GUM STORY

Stefanie tells "The Gum Story" in a visually entertaining way. This story is based on a summer camp skit.

Focus: Review the story on the DVD and learn the vocabulary below:

NEW VOCABULARY

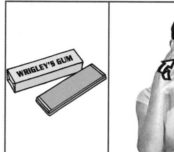

to get pleasure from, to have a good time, to relish, to enjoy

to call out loudly, to shout

transition: used to indicate the end of one event or activity and the beginning of the next one; "after that"; "then"

be unable to; can not do

be infatuated with
each other

to be unable to let go;
to be stuck

hasn't moved or changed; is still present

Homework 6:6

 ENTRANCES AND EXITS

Focus: Practice the direction from which the character enters and exits the scenes, and the placement of the gum. You will review the following:

• how the characters enter and exit the scene

• using the typically non-dominant hand as the dominant hand to maintain agreement and to help with the flow of the story.

• using the non-dominant hand as a reference to show where the gum lands

View and practice the following entrances and exits for each character.

The Boy

Use this diagram to help you remember the directions the boy enters and exits the scene.

> **NOTE:** The arrow is used to help you see and know what direction from your point of view as the signer (not from a viewer's perspective).

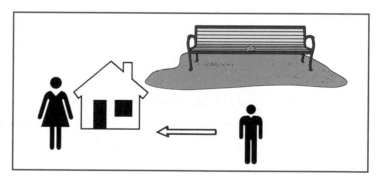

Make sure you do the following:

• indicate the bench, then as your non-dominant hand represents the bench, your dominant hand places the gum on the bench.

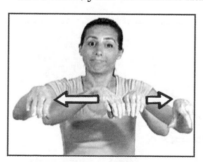

• orient and position your hand correctly to show the boy's exit.

The Man

Use this diagram to help you remember the directions the man enters and exits the scene.

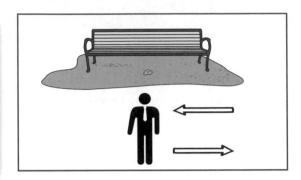

Make sure you do the following:

• indicate the ground, then use your non-dominant hand to represent the ground and your dominant hand to show the gum landing on the ground.

• show the man exiting to your right side
• orient and position your hand correctly when showing the man's entrance and exit.

The Woman

Use this diagram to help you remember the directions the woman enters and exits the scene.

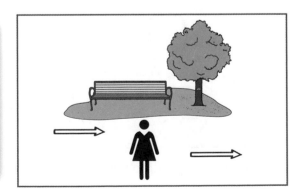

Make sure you do the following:

• take the gum off the bottom of the shoe with your non-dominant hand.

• indicate the tree, then as your dominant hand represents the tree, your non-dominant hand shows the gum landing on the tree trunk.

• show the woman exiting to your right side
• orient and position your hand correctly when showing the woman's entrance and exit.

The Couple

Use this diagram to help you remember the directions the couple enters and exits the scene.

NOTE: The arrow is used to help you see and know what direction from your point of view as the signer (not from a viewer's perspective).

Make sure you do the following:

- use your non-dominant hand to represent the tree and show the girl leaning on the tree with your dominant hand.

- use your dominant hand to show the boy leaning on the tree, and your non-dominant hand to indicate he's talking to the girl.

- indicate the bench, then use your non-dominant hand to represent the bench, as your dominant hand shows the gum landing on the bench.
- show the couple exiting to your right side
- orient and position your hand correctly when showing the couples' entrance and exit.

The Boy Again

Use this diagram to help you remember the directions the boy enters and exits the scene.

> **NOTE:** The arrow is used to help you see and know what direction from your point of view as the signer (not from a viewer's perspective).

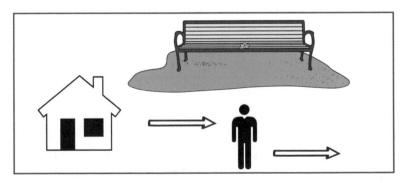

Make sure you do the following:
- pick up the gum from bench and put it into your mouth.
- show the boy exiting toward your right side.
- orient and position your hand correctly when showing the boy exit.

Homework 6:7

ONE-PERSON ROLE SHIFT—MANNER OF WALKING AND BECOMING UNSTUCK

Focus: Practice one-person role shift to describe each character's manner of walking (+ attitude) and becoming unstuck (+ reaction).

One-person role shift is used by the narrator to show how the character behaves. The narrator becomes the character, taking on his/her actions, manners and feelings. For example, in "The Gum Story," the narrator shifts to become each character showing his/her manner of walk, and his/her attempts at becoming unstuck from the gum. Effective role shift involves both your body and your eyes. Your eye gaze should look as if you are "truly" looking at the place or thing you are interacting with.

 View and practice the following scenes using one-person role shift.

The Man

Become the man and show his:
- *Manner of walk:* shuffling along with a serious, prudish attitude
- *Becoming unstuck*
  - three attempts. On the second attempt, the man signs CAN'T, and on the third try, he gets unstuck. Include changes in facial expression for each attempt.
  - looks disgusted as he picks gum (two times) off his pants and molds the gum into a ball.

The Woman

Become the woman and show her:

• *Manner of walk:* walking arrogantly with a prim, snobbish attitude

• *Becoming unstuck*

  -three attempts. Include changes in facial expression for each attempt.

  -looks disgusted—looks around to see if anyone is looking as she picks the gum off the bottom of her shoe and molds the gum into a ball.

The Couple

Become the couple and show their:

• *Manner of walk:* two of them walking romantically with an infatuated attitude

• *Becoming unstuck*

  -at the second attempt, the young man signs STUCK then with the help of his other hand manages to become unstuck. Include changes in facial expression.

  -looks disgusted as he picks the gum piece by piece off his right hand (two times) and molds the gum into a ball.

The Boy and His Mother 1

In the beginning of the story, Stefanie establishes that the mother is to the left of the boy by using role shift to show the mother yelling from the left side. To role shift to the mother, look to your right (where the boy is established). To shift roles to the boy, look to the left (where the mother is).

The Boy and His Mother 2

Near the end of the story the boy refers to his mother when he checks to his left side to be sure mom isn't watching. To do this, sign "My mom isn't looking at me," using your left hand to represent the mother, while at the same time shaking your head.

> **NOTE:** To role shift, turn your head just enough to complete the shift but not so much that the listener cannot see your facial expressions. Do not move your feet to make the shift. Only your shoulders and head turn slightly.

Homework 6:8

STORY COHESION

Focus: Practice elements needed to tell a story well.

• transitions (raised brows)

• pauses

• engaging the audience

Transitions

Use *raised brows* to signal the beginning of a new segment.

View. "Transitions" from "The Gum Story." A number will appear on screen to point out when Stefanie uses the transition in the story (listed below). Practice raising your brows to introduce each character.

1.

introduces the boy

2.

the mother calling

3.

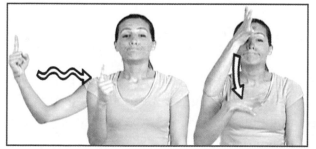

the man

4.

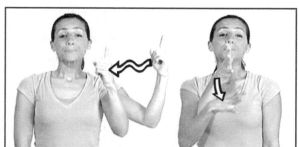

the woman

5.

the couple

6.

the boy again

Pauses

Transitions are used to begin a scene and pauses are used to end the scene. Notice how Stefanie comes to a full rest (hands down at her side) before introducing the next character.

Engaging the Audience

To tell the story well, you must engage your audience. One way to do this is to make deliberate eye contact with your audience and maintain the eye contact throughout the story. With eye contact, the listener is more attentive to the story. The only time you should break eye contact with the audience is when you role shift to a character. If you are telling the story to a camera, imagine the camera is your audience and remember the only time you can look away from the camera is when you are using role shift.

Day of Filming

On the day of the filming, please adhere to the following:

• Wear solid color clothes.

• If your hair tends to fall into your eyes, pin it back or wear a ponytail.

• Don't wear hats (unless it has no brim) because of the shadows hiding your face.

• You should have nothing in your mouth – no candy or gum while filming. If you have something in your mouth you run the risk of not executing the "face grammar" correctly, possibly resulting in a lower grade.

Homework 6:9

💿 THE GALLAUDET AND CLERC STORY

Tyrone tells this historical tale about how the founders of the first school for the Deaf met.

NEW VOCABULARY

phrase used to begin a story

Thomas Gallaudet's name sign

to amuse oneself by taking part in a game or sport; engage in recreation, to play

to feel the need of; to desire; to want

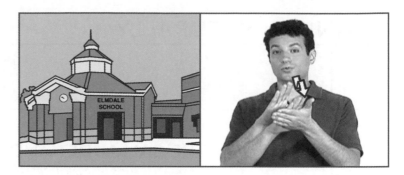

to say you don't have
something, or there is none,
or something doesn't exist

to reach one's destination;
come to a place; arrive

to search for; to hunt for

to locate something after a search

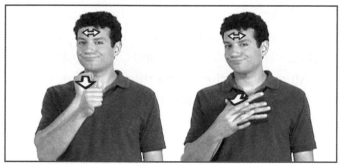

to not care for something; not like

Laurent Clerc's name sign

to set up; to establish; to form a system or institution

the first of its kind

Homework 6:10

TWO-PERSON ROLE SHIFT IN NARRATIVES

Focus: Practice two-person role shift to show the conversation between characters

In "The Gallaudet and Clerc Story," Tyrone uses two-person role shift to show the exchange between the Deaf girl and Thomas Gallaudet, and between Thomas Gallaudet and Laurent Clerc. First, Tyrone establishes the location of the characters, one on the left and the other on the right, and then shifts his body to assume the role of the character.

 View and practice the following scenes using two-person role shift.

Gallaudet and the Girl

The Deaf girl is on Tyrone's left and Gallaudet is on his right. Tyrone orients his body so it is consistent with the placement of Gallaudet and looks down to the left (at the girl) when signing. Likewise, when it is the girl's turn to respond, Tyrone looks up to the right (at Gallaudet).

(as Gallaudet)

(as the girl)

Gallaudet and Clerc

In this scene, Gallaudet is on Tyrone's left and Clerc is on his right. Tyrone orients his body so it is consistent with the placement of Gallaudet and looks to the right (at Clerc) when signing as Gallaudet. Likewise, when Clerc talks to Gallaudet, Tyrone looks to the left (at Gallaudet) when signing as Clerc.

(as Gallaudet)

(as Clerc)

Homework 6:11

MAINTAINING SPATIAL AGREEMENT

Focus: Practice maintaining spatial agreement when referring to established locations.

Establish America, England, and France in three different locations in the signing space according to how you see them on a world map and refer to them in the story.

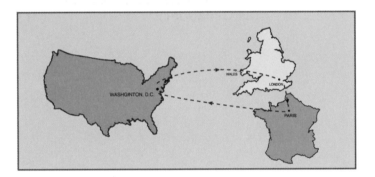

When you retell the story, maintain spatial agreement between these locations as Gallaudet moves from place to place.

View. Practice the following scenes until you can maintain spatial agreement among the locations. Remember to take the signer's perspective when establishing the countries' locations in the signing space.

America to England

England to France

France to America

NOTE: Note the use of spatial agreement when Tyrone orients the sign for "teach" to agree with the established locations of Gallaudet and Clerc.

Clerc teaching Gallaudet

Gallaudet teaching Clerc

Homework 6:12

STORY COHESION

Focus: Practice elements needed to tell a story well.

• transitions (raised brows)

• pauses

• engaging the audience

Transitions

Use *raised brows* to signal the beginning of a new scene.

View. A number will appear on screen to point out when Tyrone uses the transition in the story (see below). Practice raising your brows to introduce each scene:

1.

begins the story

2.

introduces Gallaudet

3.

upon arriving in England

4.

then, he heard about

5.

upon arriving in France

6.

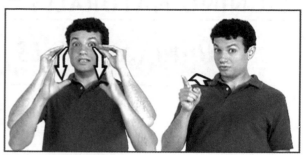

introduces Clerc

7.

the men

8.

upon arriving in America

Engaging the Audience

To tell the story well, you must engage your audience. One way to do this is to make deliberate eye contact with your audience and maintain the eye contact throughout the story. With eye contact, the listener is more attentive to the story. The only time you should break eye contact with the audience is when you role shift to a character. If you are telling the story to a camera, imagine the camera is your audience and remember the only time you can look away from the camera is when you are using role shift.

Day of Filming

On the day of the filming, please adhere to the following:

• Wear solid color clothes.

• If your hair tends to fall into your eyes, pin it back or wear a ponytail.

• Don't wear hats (unless it has no brim) because of the shadows hiding aa your face.

• You should have nothing in your mouth – no candy or gum while filming. If you have something in your mouth you run the risk of not executing the "face grammar " correctly, possibly resulting in a lower grade.

Homework 6:13

CHILDHOOD STORIES: "WRONG NAME"

Watch Michelle tell this story, then answer the following questions.

1. Where did the parents go for their vacation? For how long?

2. Where did the children stay?

3. What did the parents bring back for each child?

4. What did Michelle do to her hat? What did she use?

5. What happened when she looked in the mirror?

6. How did her mother explain the problem?

7. What does Michelle understand now that she didn't back then?

8. This story takes place over how many days?

Answers are given in class.

New Vocabulary

sometime in the past; long time ago

one long week

enthusiastic, excited with anticipation

transition: the following day

wrong, not correct

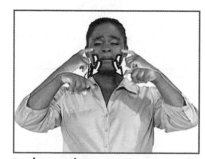

to burst into tears

wh-word: ask what is the matter

**to chuckle; to laugh
quietly to oneself**

**not in working condition;
broken**

transition: now

to realize; to understand

Transitions

What follows are a few examples of transitions used by Michelle to move the story along. Watch the story again to see how she used these transitions in the context of the story. Notice she raises her brows when signing the transition.

Transitions using time signs:

"After a long week, our parents returned..."

"The day after, I got my sombrero..."

"Now, as an adult..."

⊙ CHILDHOOD STORIES: "IF ONLY I COULD FLY"

Watch Priscilla tell this story then answer the following questions.

1. What did Priscilla want to do?

2. What did Priscilla's mom want Priscilla to help her with?

3. After Mom caught Priscilla eating the cookies, where did she put the cookies?

4. How was Priscilla able to reach the cookies?

5. When she heard her mother coming, what did she do?

6. What happened to Priscilla?

7. This story takes place over how long a period of time?

Answers are given in class.

New Vocabulary

to do repeatedly in order
to become proficient

to help, to aid, to assist

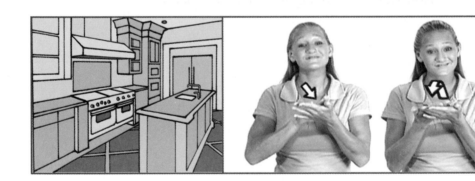

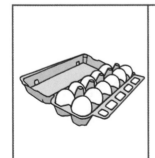

tasty, scrumptious, delicious

to remain in anticipation;
to wait for

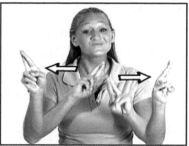
transition: to be ready for
the next step

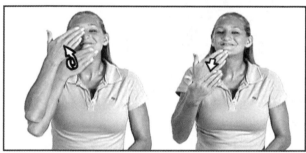
to smell something good

to express an apology;
sorry

transition: a sudden
unexpected change

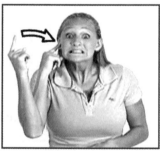
transition: to hear
something unexpectedly

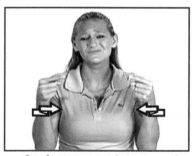
to feel or experience pain

to bring a person or thing to a
place, i.e. hospital

Transitions

What follows are a few examples of transitions used by Priscilla to move the story along. Watch the story again to see how she used these transitions in the context of the story. Notice she raises her brows when signing the transition.

Transitions using time signs:

"Then, one day, when I was five..."

"By then, I realized I couldn't fly"

Other transitions:

"When the cookies were ready..."

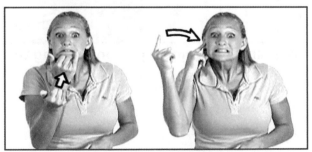

"All of a sudden, I heard my mom..."

SIGNS FOR SEEING

Joey signs a narrative using all four signs below. Watch the narrative and find the signs.

A

to search for;
to hunt for

B

to watch something
without being an
active participant
i.e., a game, a movie,
people walking by

C

the act of looking
at something or
someone

D

to notice; to
witness; to see

NOTE: Sign "B"
above cannot
be used in a
command, i.e.,
to tell someone
to "Look at me"
or "Look at that!"

Exercise

Identify the best sign(s) to use (A, B, C, or D) to translate the sentences below. Put the corresponding letter next to the sentence. See example below.

Example: __B__   I enjoy watching people go by.

1. _____ I went to see a movie yesterday.

2. _____ Watch me dance.

3. _____ I looked everywhere for my keys and I can't find them.

4. _____ Watch her make a flower.

5. _____ Can you see me clearly?

6. _____ I enjoy watching football on Sunday.

Answers are given in class.

Homework 6:14

CHILDHOOD STORIES: "A TRUE FISH STORY"

Watch Norman tell this story then answer the following questions.

1. What did the family like to do?

2. When did the father want to go fishing?

3. When did the boys get up?

4. What did they eat for breakfast?

5. What happened when the boys threw the egg shells in the water?

6. How did the boys catch the fish?

7. How many fishes did they catch?

8. How long did they wait for their dad to return to camp?

9. How many fishes did the father catch?

10. What happened when the father saw the fish the boys caught?

11. This story takes place over how many days?

Answers are given in class.

New Vocabulary

enthusiastic; excited with
anticipation

to put on one's own clothes;
to get dressed

to move or act with haste;
to rush; to act quickly;
to hurry

all being counted or
or included; in all;
altogether

to be glad, pleased,
content

to become mad or upset

Transitions

What follows are a few examples of transitions used by Norman to move the story along. Watch the story again to see how he used these transitions in the context of the story. Notice he raises his brows when signing the transition.

Transitions using time signs:

"Last night...."

"Early in the morning, at 4 A.M."

Other transitions:

"Upon arriving at the campgrounds..."

SIGNS FOR NEGATING

Isias signs a narrative using all four signs below.
Watch the narrative and find the signs.

A

not able to do
something because
something is
preventing you

B

to politely tell
someone not to
do something;
to caution against
doing something

C

to say something
is not...; to deny
something

D

no person or
thing; none

NOTE: Sign "A"
above is not used
to describe one's
lack of skills.

Exercise

Identify the best sign(s) to use (A, B, C, or D) to translate the
sentences below. Put the corresponding letter next to the sentence.

1. _____ I don't like waiting.

2. _____ I couldn't open the lid to the jar.

3. _____ Don't run through the house.

4. _____ Don't stare.

5. _____ I couldn't find the flashlight.

6. _____ There isn't any coffee left.

The negative sign should be at the end of your ASL sentence.
First, set up the topic or subject with raised eyebrows, then
comment. Example: In the sentence "I don't like waiting," begin
with "waiting," then tell you don't like to.

Challenge Yourself
Identify the topic of the sentences above, and then try translating
the sentence using the negative sign at the end.

Answers are given in class.

Homework 6:15

 CHILDHOOD STORIES: "I WANNA BE DIFFERENT"

Watch Melinda tell this story, then answer the following questions.

Narrative Structure
Background

1. After introducing the sign for "rooster," what phrase did Melinda use to open the story? (memorize and show in class)

2. Summarize the information in this portion of the story.

Body

3. What transition did Melinda use to begin the Body of the story? (memorize and show in class)

4. Summarize the information in this portion of the story.

Conclusion

5. What transition did Melinda use to conclude the story? (memorize and show in class)

6. Summarize the information in this portion of the story.

Check the Box

This story takes place over several days. In each clip, and identify how the signs below are used within the clip. Do the signs function as a transition, or have they been modified to show the activity continues for some time? Check the appropriate box.

1. ❑ transition   ❑ modified verb

2. ❑ transition   ❑ modified verb

3. ❑ transition   ❑ modified verb

4. ❑ transition   ❑ modified verb

5. ❑ transition   ❑ modified verb

Answers are given in class.

> **NOTE:** Since these two signs are made similarly, to determine the meaning of the sign you must look at the sign in context.

to be unlike; different   **transition: however, yet, but**

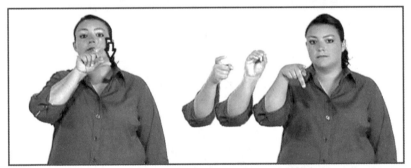

a contagious disease usually in young children, characterized by fever and red spots (chicken pox)

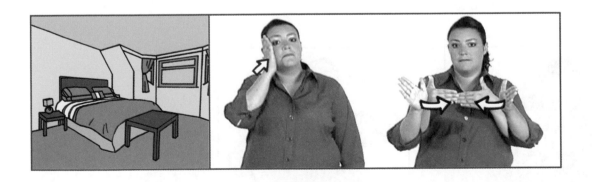

to mock, laugh at

a few days later

transition: later on; subsequently

Transitions

What follows are a few examples of transitions used by Melinda to move the story along. Watch the story again to see how she used these transitions in the context of the story. Notice she raises her brows when signing the transition.

Transitions using time signs:

in the past; long ago   one day

a few days later

Other transitions:

however, yet, but

Modifying the verb to move the story along:

looking over

mocking and laughing at someone "for a while"

SIGNS FOR TALKING

Iva signs a narrative using all four signs below.
Watch the narrative and find the signs.

A

to express vocally;
to speak

B

to converse in an
informal manner;
to chat

C

to state something;
to say

D

to inform me; to tell
me; to notify me

Exercise

Identify the best sign(s) to use (A, B, C, or D) to translate the
sentences below. Put the corresponding letter next to the sentence.

1. _____ When I was little, my teachers said I talked too much in
class.

2. _____ I enjoyed talking with her.

3. _____ My aunt mentioned to us she used to live in France.

4. _____ My grandmother mentioned she liked Hershey's
chocolate candy.

5. _____ While talking with her, I discovered she and I both like
Elvis.

6. _____ I started signing when I was 1 year old. I started talking
when I was 2 years old.

Answers are given in class.

Homework 6:16

 CHILDHOOD STORIES: "GHOST IN MY ROOM"

Watch Cinnie tell this story, then answer the following questions.

Narrative Structure
Background

1. What phrase did Cinnie use to open the story?
(memorize and show in class)

2. Summarize the information in this portion of the story.

Body

3. What transition did Cinnie use to begin the Body of the story?
(memorize and show in class)

4. Summarize the information in this portion of the story.

Conclusion

5. What transition did Cinnie use to conclude the story?
(memorize and show in class)

6. Summarize the information in this portion of the story.

Check the Box

This story takes place over several days. In each clip identify how the signs below are used within the clip. Do the signs function as a transition, or have they been modified to show the activity continues for some time? Check the appropriate box.

1. ❑ transition ❑ modified verb

2. ❑ transition ❑ modified verb

3. ❑ transition ❑ modified verb

4. ❑ transition ❑ modified verb

5. ❑ transition ❑ modified verb

Answers are given in class.

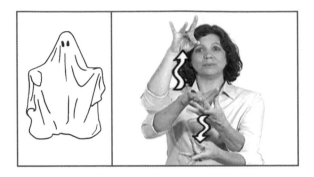

friendly, ready to be a friend

malicious, mean-spirited

to see for oneself; to check something out

to chuckle, to laugh quietly to oneself

to be afraid; scared

untidy, disorganized, messy

"how nice," "how cool," "how convenient"

Transitions

What follows are a few examples of transitions used by Cinnie to move the story along. Watch the story again to see how she used these transitions in the context of the story. Notice she raises her brows when signing the transition.

Transitions using time signs:

"One day when...."

"later on...."

Other transitions:

"I got an idea to...."

"then...."

Modifying the verb to move the story along

playing for a while

cooking for a while

cleaning for a while

Homework 6:17

GUIDELINES: TELLING YOUR OWN CHILDHOOD STORY

Your project is to tell a childhood story.

In choosing your story, consider the following:
• the story should be about 3-4 minutes long.
• the story should not center on a sound, a play on words (pun), or the meaning of a particular word.
• there should be no more than three characters in the story.
• choose an incident that can be communicated using what we have learned in class.
• the story must be told in the first person, i.e., told from your point of view.

You will tell the final version of your story on _____
(date)

Narrative Structure

Your story should follow the structure below:

NARRATIVE STRUCTURE

I. Background –
• begin with an opening phrase
• give relevant background – who, when, where, and/or what happened before

II. Body –
• begin with a transition
• use role shift (at least three turns in the exchange)
• integrate feelings and reactions
• use the "object, action" word order
• use transitions and modified verbs to move the story along

III. Conclusion –
• begin with a transition
• comment what you learned and/or what has happened since

Rehearsing the Story

Rehearse your story until you are completely comfortable.

• memorize the opening. It helps you get over the nervousness at the beginning.

• memorize the conclusion. It gives you the needed confidence to wrap up your story effectively.

Telling the Story

Tell your story in a sitting position.

• articulate your signs clearly and correctly.

• move only your head, eyes, and shoulder when role shifting, not your whole body.

• pace your story and engage your listeners.

• make eye contact with everyone in the group.

• do not end your story with an announcement that you are done.

Your audience should know that you are done by the way you wind down the story and bring it to a close.

Grading Criteria

You will be graded based on how well you:

• followed the narrative structure

• incorporated the essential language elements

• formed your signs correctly and used a good range of vocabulary

• used appropriate amount of details and that made sense

• were able to get the meaning across

• engaged the audience

LANGUAGE ELEMENTS

Review the following elements and think of ways to incorporate them into telling your story.

Role Shift

To show a conversation between an adult and child, you can use "up and down" and/or side to side role shift. Watch the conversational exchanges from the story "Wrong Name" between Michelle and her mother. The scenes are shown in slow motion.

Role shift 1: Michelle is upset her name is spelled wrong in the mirror

Role shift 2: her mother assures Michelle the name on the sombrero is spelled correctly

Mom looks down at Michelle (on Mom's left)

Michelle looks up at Mom (on her right)

Notice how Michelle directs her mom's attention to the (imaginary) mirror.

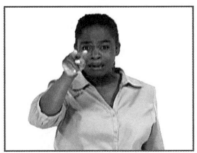

Michelle tells her mom to look (at the mirror)

Mom looks (at the mirror)

Word Order

To describe an action involving an object, follow this word order:
- name object (use raised brows)
- describe the action.

Examples below are from "If Only I Could Fly." Notice that Priscilla uses raised brows when signing the object.

Word Order 1. Priscilla signs "cape" and describes "tying it on"

Word Order 2. Priscilla signs "box" and describes "jumping off the box"

Word Order 3. Priscilla signs "egg" and describes "cracking eggs open"

Word Order 4. Priscilla signs "plate" and describes "transferring cookies to the plate"

Word Order 5. Priscilla signs "drawers" and describes "opening them"

Word Order 6. Priscilla signs "cookies" and describes "eating them"

A story takes place over a period of time. To move a story along, modifying the verbs and using transitions are helpful.

Modified Verbs

One way to move the story along (by showing the passage of time) is to modify the verbs. Watch video examples to review how these verbs are modified.

Modified Verbs 1. Michelle modifies this verb by exaggerating and repeating the sign.

Modified Verbs 2. Norman modifies this verb by repeating the sign with a circular movement

Modified Verbs 3. Priscilla modifies this verb by prolonging the sign.

Modified Verbs 4. Norman modifies this verb by repeating the sign.

Modified Verbs 5. Priscilla modifies this verb by repeating the sign.

⊙ *Transitions*

Another way to move the story along is to use transitions. Watch
video examples to observe how and where these transitions occur.

Transition 1

"the following day"

Transition 2

"one day"

Transition 3

"a few days later"

Transition 4

"by now"

Transition 5

"to be ready for (the next step)"

Transition 6

"then, after that"

Transition 7

"all of a sudden..."

Transition 8

"the idea/thought came to me..."

ASL learners often confuse the signs below when they want to express the concept "later."

This sign is appropriate when translating sentences like "I was **late** for class."

"past the expected due time/date; to be late"

These signs are correctly used when translating sentences like "We will do that **later**."

"(will do) in a while"

This sign is a transition that moves a story along and used correctly in this context: "After I graduated from college, I got a job. **Later** on, I quit my job and traveled the world."

"subsequently, after some time"

So, the next time the word **"later"** pops up in your mind while you are signing, choose the correct sign to fit the context of your message and your message will come across smoothly!

Strategies to Get the Meaning Across

As you develop your story, you may need to communicate concepts that the class has not learned signs for. These two strategies help you do that:

> **STRATEGY: DESCRIBE THE CONCEPT**
> If it's an object, describe and show how it is used.

To do this, be sure to look directly at your audience, nod, raise brows and describe the concept, then continue with your story.

You may have noticed signers using this sign as well to signal they are about to describe a concept.

sign used to signal the concept is something familiar

View. Observe how each signer signals a concept is about to be described and then proceeds to describe the object.

Strategy 1. Norman describes a hook and line.
Strategy 2. Priscilla describes the kitchen drawers.
Strategy 3. Michelle describes a sombrero.

If just describing a concept is not sufficient, and you need to use a sign that may not be familiar to your audience, use this next strategy.

STRATEGY: TO INTRODUCE A "KEY" SIGN
If a sign is "critical" to understanding the point of the story, it is best to introduce the sign before you go on. In this case, follow this sequence:
- state the new sign
- explain its meaning (with raised brows)
- then, restate the new sign

View. Observe how the signs for these concepts are introduced and restated as "key" signs for their stories.

Strategy 4. Melinda introduces the sign for this concept.

Strategy 5. Cinnie introduces the sign for this concept.

Strategy 6. Cinnie introduces the sign for this concept "untidy, disorganized, messy."

Parts of the House

These signs may be useful for your story. Watch Michelle demonstrate these signs.

BACKYARD

BR

BATH

KIT

LR

DR

Narrative Structure

Watch all the childhood stories again to review the phrases used to:

• begin the "background"
• begin the "body"
• begin the "conclusion"

Select and adapt those that are most suitable for your story.

Enjoy telling your childhood story. Break a leg! Or some fingers!

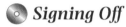

Signing Off

The actors have final messages for you. Watch them and enjoy.

SIGNING NATURALLY

Classroom Exercises Units 1–5

Exercise 1:1

ABOVE, BELOW, AND INSIDE

Instructions: Add shapes, names, or numbers to the shapes in the top box. Limit your additions to above, inside, or below the existing shapes. Do not add anything to the left or right of the shapes.

Describe to your partner what you have done. First, identify which shape, then describe your additions. Your partner will draw your additions.

Add to the shapes here (above, below, or inside only).

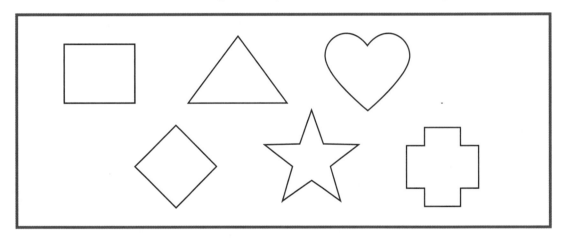

Draw your partner's additions here.

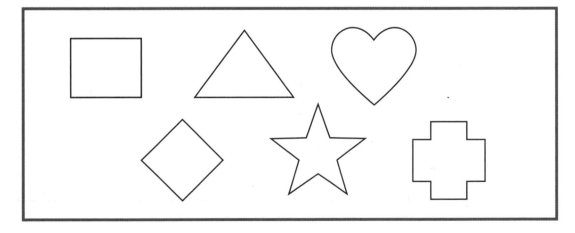

When done, compare drawings with your partner.

Exercise 2:1

LANGUAGE BACKGROUNDS

Instructions. Your partner will narrate about a person's "Language Biography." When she or he is done, you may ask questions for clarification. Fill in the blanks below. Then repeat the information back to your partner to confirm the information you recorded.

1. name: _____

   languages she or he grew up with: _____

2. **high school time**

   -other language(s) learned:_____

   -number of years:_____

   -how much language remembered:

   |——|——|——|——|——|
   100%   0%

3) **college time**

   -other language(s) learned:_____

   -number of years:_____

   -how much language remembered:

   |——|——|——|——|——|
   100%   0%

4) **present time**
   -other language(s) currently learning:_____

   -level of difficulty:

   |——|——|——|——|——|
   very difficult   *very easy*

Exercise 2:2

DESCRIBE A COMBINATION OF SHAPES

Instructions. Draw your own combination of shapes in Grid A. When done, describe your shapes to your partner. They will draw the shapes you describe in Grid B.

Grid A – Draw your own combinations here.

1.	2.	3.
4.	5.	6.

Grid B – Draw your partner's shapes here.

1.	2.	3.
4.	5.	6.

Exercise 2:3

IDENTIFY OTHERS

Instructions: First, pick six students in Classroom A. Add names and two pieces of information (personal information, language background, leisure activity, likes or dislikes). Use the names from page 68. When ready, identify the student in the picture, give his or her name and the two facts (vocabulary used to identify the student does not count as facts). Your partner will record the information in Classroom B. When done, switch roles and record your partner's information.

Classroom A. Add names and two pieces of information to six students in this picture.

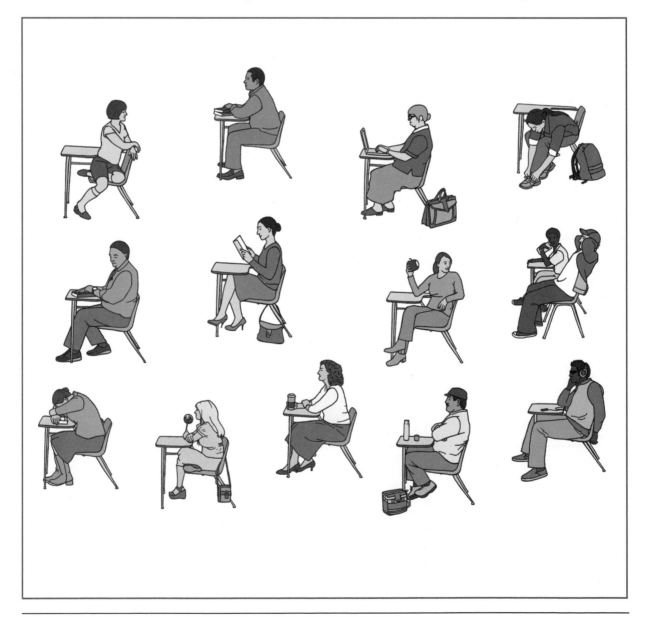

Classroom B. Record the information given by your partner here.

Dialogue

A: Identify a person by
  - their gender and two or more of the following:
    their appearance,
    body position,
    or action
B: Acknowledge
A: Give the person's name and state their favorite leisure activity

Exercise 2:4

WHO LIKES WHAT?

Instructions: Go around the classroom and find students who like doing one of the leisure activities below. Write that person's name in the blank under the activity. Make sure to sign your question and not rely on pointing to the picture!

Exercise 2:5

NAMES

Instructions: Pick one of the names below as your name for this activity.

Write it here: _____

Now go around the room introducing yourself to other students with your "new" name. Follow the dialogue format you have learned in class. (The activity ends when you have met someone with each of these names or if you have met everyone in class). Cross these names off as you meet someone with that "adopted" name.

Sean	Naomi	Tom	Seena	Carl
Rita	Ian	Carrie	Danny	Edna
Bobby	Kurt	Matt	Moe	Alex

Exercise 3:1

"DOWN" LETTERS CROSSWORD PUZZLE

Instructions: The teacher tells you where to put the word she or he fingerspells. Fill in the grid below. Remember to take the signer's perspective to determine the placement of the word.

Exercise 3:2

FILL IN THE SQUARES

Instructions: Your teacher will identify one of the nine squares below, then ask you a question. Fill in the appropriate square with your answer.

Exercise 3:3

FIND MY PET

How to Begin

- You and your partner decide who will take grid "Blue" and who will take grid "Green." (see page 386).
- Then, shade the squares inside your grid to represent each of these four pets. You can fill in the squares vertically or horizontally, but not diagonally.

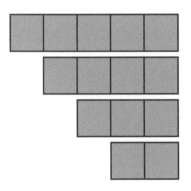

Shade five squares to represent the dog

Shade four squares to represent the cat

Shade three squares to represent the bird

Shade two squares to represent the fish

How to Play

- The objective is to locate all your partner's pets before they find yours.
- Begin by choosing two numbers from your partner's grid–one from the top row and one from the column to the left, and ask if that square is a "hit." Your opponent will check the point where your numbers intersect and tell you if you hit or missed a pet.
- If you make a "hit," shade in the square on your grid so you can keep track of where the pets are located.
- If you miss, mark the square with an "X" so you don't repeat those numbers the next time.
- Continue the game, taking turns signing out numbers until you have discovered all of the pets and can identify which pet is located where. The only way to know what pet is located where is by the number of shaded squares it occupies.
- The first person to identify where all of the pets are located is the winner.

When your partner gives you two numbers from their grid, and they "hit" a part of your "pet," use this phrase:

If your partner's two numbers do not hit any part of your pets, use this phrase:

Sample Grid

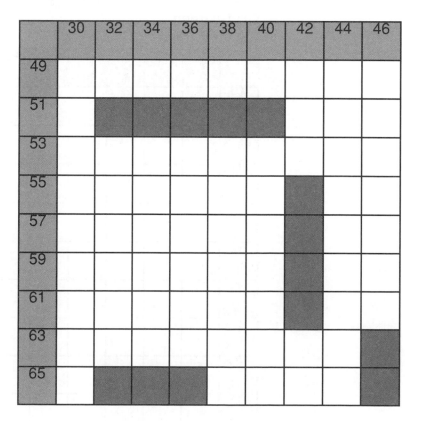

	30	32	34	36	38	40	42	44	46
49									
51		■	■	■	■				
53									
55							■		
57							■		
59							■		
61							■		
63									■
65		■	■		■				■

Grid "Blue"

	30	32	34	36	38	40	42	44	46
49									
51									
53									
55									
57									
59									
61									
63									
65									

Grid "Green"

	30	32	34	36	38	40	42	44	46
49									
51									
53									
55									
57									
59									
61									
63									
65									

Exercise 3:4

DISCUSSING LIVING SITUATIONS

Instructions: Interview two (2) students in your class and write down the information in the spaces below.

1. Name:_____

2. Lives in (city): _____

3. Near/area: _____(optional)

4. Type of residence: _____ size: _____

5. Live with: _____

6. Pets (type, how many): _____

7. Work at:_____

8. How do they get to work: _____

9. How long it takes to get to work from home: _____

10. How do they get to class: _____

11. How long does it take to get to class: _____

---

1. Name:_____

2. Lives in (city): _____

3. Near/area: _____(optional)

4. Type of residence: _____ size: _____

5. Live with: _____

6. Pets (type, how many): _____

7. Work at:_____

8. How do they get to work: _____

9. How long it takes to get to work from home: _____

10. How do they get to class: _____

11. How long does it take to get to class: _____

Exercise 4:1

QUICK SURVEY

Instructions. Interview four students and write down their information in the space provided.

STUDENT 1				
STUDENT 2				
STUDENT 3				
STUDENT 4				

When finished, pick one name and prepare a short narrative using his/her answers. Begin your narrative with the person's name (don't forget to point out him/her before telling his/her answers).

Exercise 5:1

LISA'S WEEK

For the purpose of this activity, today is Wednesday, and the calendar represents one week only.

"TODAY"

SUN	MON	TUES	WED	THURS	FRI	SAT

Dialogue 1

Take turns asking each other about activities Lisa has scheduled.

> **Signer A:** Ask when Lisa did/will do a certain activity
>
> **Signer B:** Tell when

Exercise 5:2

JOY'S WEEK

For the purpose of this activity, today is Wednesday, and the calendar represents one week only.

"TODAY"

Dialogue 2

Take turns asking each other questions about what Joy has planned on a particular day.

> **Signer A:** Ask what Joy did/will do on a certain day
>
> **Signer B:** Tell the activity

Exercise 5:3

ARE YOU DONE...?

Select any 6 activities below by putting a ✓ in the small box.

Now, pair up with a partner. Take turns asking each other if s/he has done an activity. If you have a ✓ in the box, answer affirmatively (done). If the box is unmarked, answer negatively (not done). Follow the dialogue format.

> **Signer A:** Ask if B has done the chore
>
> **Signer B:** Affirm or negate

Exercise 5:4

SEQUENCING TWO ACTIVITIES

Copy the calendar on the board. Now fill in the schedule with two activities you did or will do for each day (six days past previous and the next six days including today).

Sun	Mon	Tues	Weds	Thurs	Fri	Sat

Your Partner's Schedule

Ask your partner what s/he did/will do on a certain day.
Fill in the calendar below.

Sun	Mon	Tues	Weds	Thurs	Fri	Sat

Exercise 5:5

HOW OFTEN?

Each person takes a turn asking a question to the group. Everyone records the answer given and the person asking volunteers his/her answer as well. Based on the answers, write the letter that corresponds to the correct frequency chart next to the activity. For example, if your partner said he or she went to the video store once a month, you would put the letter **A** next to the picture.

> **Signer A:** Ask how frequently group members do a chore/errand
>
> **Signer B (everyone):** Tell how often
>
> **A:** (record answer)

Frequency Charts

A.

S	M	T	W	T	F	S
1	2	3	4	5	6	7
8	9	10	11	12	13	14
15	16	17	18	**19**	20	21
22	23	24	25	26	27	28
29	30	31				

B.

S	M	T	W	T	F	S
1	2	3	4	5	6	7
8	9	10	11	**12**	13	14
15	16	17	18	19	20	21
22	23	24	25	**26**	27	28
29	30	31				

C.

S	M	T	W	T	F	S
1	**2**	3	4	5	6	7
8	9	10	11	12	13	14
15	**16**	17	18	19	20	21
22	23	24	25	26	27	28
29	**30**	31				

D.

S	M	T	W	T	F	S
1	2	3	**4**	5	6	7

E.

S	M	T	W	T	F	S
1	2	**3**	4	**5**	6	7

F.

S	M	T	W	T	F	S
1	2	**3**	**4**	5	6	7

G.

S	M	T	W	T	F	S
1	**2**	**3**	**4**	**5**	**6**	**7**

H.

S	M	T	W	T	F	S
1	2	3	4	5	6	7

	PARTNER'S NAME	PARTNER'S NAME	YOUR NAME

F R E Q U E N C Y

	PARTNER'S NAME	PARTNER'S NAME	YOUR NAME

F R E Q U E N C Y

F R E Q U E N C Y

F R E Q U E N C Y

F R E Q U E N C Y

F R E Q U E N C Y

F R E Q U E N C Y

F R E Q U E N C Y

F R E Q U E N C Y

F R E Q U E N C Y

SIGNING NATURALLY

Exercise 5:6

FILL IN THE CALENDAR

Your teacher will give you instructions to fill in the calendar below. First, find the day of the week mentioned. Then draw a shape, or write in an activity in the space and circle the time of day.

Sun	Mon	Tues	Weds	Thurs	Fri	Sat
AM PM EVE	AM PM EVE	AM PM EVE	AM PM EVE	AM PM EVE	AM PM EVE	AM PM EVE
			TODAY			
AM PM EVE	AM PM EVE	AM PM EVE	AM PM EVE	AM PM EVE	AM PM EVE	AM PM EVE
AM PM EVE	AM PM EVE	AM PM EVE	AM PM EVE	AM PM EVE	AM PM EVE	AM PM EVE

HOMEWORK 1:2, CARDINAL NUMBERS 1–10
Circle the Number, p. 7

1.	3	(6)	9
2.	(7)	8	9
3.	3	6	(9)
4.	7	(8)	9
5.	(3)	6	9
6.	7	(8)	9

HOMEWORK 1:3, FIST LETTERS
Circle the Letter, p. 13

1.	ae	ao	(as)
2.	sa	(so)	se
3.	sn	(st)	sm
4.	mi	(ni)	ti
5.	mi	ei	(si)
6.	ei	ie	(ai)
7.	(en)	on	sn
8.	(ta)	sa	na
9.	oe	(os)	oa
10.	ea	(oa)	os

HOMEWORK 1:5, WH-WORD QUESTIONS
Minidialogues Activity, p. 18

Minidialogue 1: <u>Where is the name "Tom"?</u>

Minidialogue 2: <u>The name "Sue" belongs to who?</u>

Minidialogue 3: <u>What number comes after 5?</u>

Minidialogue 4: <u>What letter comes after D?</u>

Minidialogue 5: <u>Who is Sam?</u>

Minidialogue 6: <u>Where is the missing shape ✗ ?</u>

HOMEWORK 1:6, CARDINAL NUMBERS 11–15
Circle the Number, p. 22

1.	1	②	11	12
2.	2	3	⑫	13
3.	4	5	14	⑮
4.	①	2	11	12
5.	2	3	12	⑬
6.	4	⑤	14	15
7.	1	2	⑪	12
8.	2	③	12	13
9.	④	5	14	15
10.	①	2	11	12
11.	2	3	12	⑬
12.	4	5	⑭	15

HOMEWORK 1:7, FIST LETTER NAMES
Circle the Name, p. 24

1. (Tami)   Tim   Tom
2. Nina   Tina   (Ina)
3. Tami   (Sina)   Sami
4. Mae   (Moe)   Mona
5. (Naomi)   Toni   Stan
6. Sean   Sina   (Sam)
7. Mimi   Tami   (Mia)
8. Ines   (Ina)   Ian

Cross Out the Name, p. 24

1. Tami   ~~Tim~~   Tom
2. ~~Nina~~   Tina   Ina
3. Tami   Sina   ~~Sami~~
4. ~~Mae~~   Moe   Mona
5. Naomi   ~~Toni~~   Stan
6. ~~Sean~~   Sina   Sam
7. ~~Mimi~~   Tami   Mia
8. Ines   Ina   ~~Ian~~

HOMEWORK 1:11, TEST YOUR EYE-Q
Same or Different, p. 31

	Same	Different	If different, tell what is different.			
1.	S	(D)	shape	(name)	sign	number
2.	S	(D)	shape	name	(sign)	number
3.	(S)	D	shape	name	sign	number
4.	(S)	D	shape	name	sign	number
5.	S	(D)	(shape)	name	sign	number
6.	S	(D)	shape	name	(sign)	number
7.	(S)	D	shape	name	sign	number
8.	(S)	D	shape	name	sign	number
9.	S	(D)	shape	name	sign	(number)
10.	(S)	D	shape	name	sign	number
11.	(S)	D	shape	name	sign	number
12.	S	(D)	shape	name	sign	(number)
13.	(S)	D	shape	name	sign	number
14.	S	(D)	shape	name	(sign)	number
15.	S	(D)	shape	(name)	sign	number
16.	S	(D)	shape	(name)	sign	number
17.	S	(D)	shape	name	(sign)	number
18.	(S)	D	shape	name	sign	number

UNIT 1 REVIEW
Minidiaglogues 1–3, p. 35

Minidialogue 1

What does Tom look like? <u>**the man with the white beard**</u>

Does the woman remember all the men and women's names?

<u>**No, she remembers all the men's name and just one woman's**</u>
<u>**name.**</u>

What are the two women's (the signer and the woman in the

orange jacket) names? <u>**The signer's name is Ina. The other**</u>

<u>**woman's name is Ines.**</u>

Minidialogue 2

What color does David think Michelle's shoes are? <u>**purple**</u>

The woman's shoes are the same color as whose shoes?

<u>**the dancing woman**</u>

What is that person's name? <u>**Emma**</u>

What color are David's shoes?

<u>**one shoe is black, the other shoe is brown**</u>

Minidialogue 3

What color paper does Joey ask Tyrone to take? <u>**yellow**</u>

What does Joey ask Tyrone to draw? <u>**A rectangle with a horizontal**</u>
<u>**line in the middle with a heart with the number 7 inside the heart**</u>
<u>**under the middle line**</u>

Where does Joey tell Tyrone to write his name? <u>**above the rectangle**</u>

What does Joey correct in Tyrone's drawing?

<u>**the number ("8" should be "7")**</u>

HOMEWORK 2:2, CARDINAL NUMBERS 16–19
Circle the Number, p. 58–59

1.	16	(17)	18	19
2.	16	17	18	(19)
3.	(16)	17	18	19
4.	16	17	(18)	19
5.	6	16	(9)	19
6.	6	(16)	9	19
7.	(6)	16	9	19
8.	6	16	9	(19)
9.	7	17	(8)	18
10.	7	(17)	8	18
11.	7	17	8	(18)
12.	(7)	17	8	18

HOMEWORK 2:3, TIC-TAC-TOE *p. 60*

Game 1

X	O	X
X	O	O
O	X	

Game 2

X	O	X
X	O	
	X	O

Game 3

O	X	O
	X	O
X		O

HOMEWORK 2:5, UP LETTER NAMES
Circle the Name, p. 68

1. Carl (Earl)
2. Dawn (Dean)
3. (Dana) Dan
4. (Cara) Cole
5. (Kurt) Burt
6. Fran (Fred)
7. (Dale) Kali
8. (Ted) Ned

9. Rima (Rita)
10. Bea (Bert)
11. (Ben) Ken
12. Mike (Mel)
13. Lilli (Lon)
14. (Ed) Di
15. (Van) Val
16. Max (Alex)

Number the Names, p. 68

1. __1__ Olin
    __3__ Eli
    __2__ Carol

2. __2__ Carl
    __1__ Edna
    __3__ Rick

3. __3__ Cara
    __1__ Kris
    __2__ Karl

4. __3__ Cole
    __2__ Burt
    __1__ Rima

HOMEWORK 2:7, CARDINAL NUMBERS 20–29
Circle the Number, p. 73

1. 23 **(24)** 25 26
2. **(20)** 21 22 27
3. 26 **(27)** 28 29
4. 23 24 **(25)** 26
5. 20 21 22 **(27)**
6. **(26)** 27 28 29
7. **(23)** 24 25 26
8. 20 21 **(22)** 27
9. 26 27 28 **(29)**
10. 23 24 25 **(26)**
11. 20 **(21)** 22 27
12. 26 27 **(28)** 29

HOMEWORK 2:10, DOUBLE LETTER NAMES
Circle the Name, p. 82

1. Libby **(Lilly)** Linny
2. Dolly Danny Donny **(Debby)**
3. Etta **(Emma)** Ella
4. Emmie Eddie Ellie **(Effie)**
5. **(Manny)** Matty Maddy

HOMEWORK 2:10, DOUBLE LETTER NAMES
Fill in the Blank, p. 82

1. Lo<u>TT</u>ie
2. Lo<u>NN</u>ie
3. Do<u>TT</u>ie
4. Do<u>NN</u>ie
5. Ki<u>TT</u>y
6. Ki<u>MM</u>y
7. Ta<u>MM</u>y
8. Ta<u>FF</u>y
9. Ke<u>LL</u>y
10. Ke<u>RR</u>y

11. Pa<u>TT</u>y
12. Pa<u>DD</u>y
13. <u>SOO</u>n
14. <u>YOO</u>n
15. W<u>ALL</u>y
16. W<u>ILL</u>y
17. Te<u>LL</u>y
18. Te<u>RR</u>y

UNIT 2 REVIEW: WHICH IS THE BEST RESPONSE?
Check the Box, p. 88

	Response 1	Response 2
1.	☑	☐
2.	☐	☑
3.	☑	☐
4.	☐	☑
5.	☐	☑

UNIT 2 REVIEW: AUTOBIOGRAPHIES, *p. 89*

Autobiography 1

Name **Billy**

Personal information: Deaf or hearing **Deaf**

Language background: **grew up with 2 languages - ASL and reading/writing English; attended Gallaudet where he studied French Sign Language for 2 years. He remembers most of the signs.**

What s/he is doing now: **has been teaching ASL at this college (here) for 4 years**

Likes/dislikes: **likes to play with his 2 dogs, also likes to talk with his students**

Favorite color: **green**

Autobiography 2

Name **Sara**

Personal information: Deaf or hearing **born hearing, became Deaf at a young age as a result of illness**

Language background: **it was difficult learning to speak English; but learning to read and write English was much easier (somewhat easy); later, as she got older, she began to learn ASL, something that she liked doing. In High School, she learned to read and write Spanish which she found to be somewhat difficult.**

Likes/dislikes: **likes to travel, likes going to France – she has seen the Eiffel Tower**

Favorite color: **blue**

Autobiography 3

Name **Emma**

Personal information: Deaf or hearing **Hearing**

Language background: **grew up with 2 languages: spoken English and ASL; did not study any language when she was in High School.**

Likes/dislikes: **likes to go camping, and hiking, enjoys fishing**

Favorite color: **red**

HOMEWORK 3:1, CONVERSATION 1
Minidialogue, p. 111

Minidialogue 1

Berkeley: who lives there <u>**Ben**</u>
   which area? <u>near the university</u>

Fremont: who lives there <u>**Darby**</u>
   which area? <u>**near the lake**</u>

Oakland: who lives there <u>**Joey**</u>
   which area? <u>**in the hills**</u>
   what can he see from his home? <u>**the city of San Francisco**</u>

What comment was made at the end of the conversation?
<u>**It is a long way from Darby's home to school here in Oakland**</u>

HOMEWORK 3:4, MOVING LETTER "Z"
Write the Word, p. 117

Fingerspelled word		Clue
1.	<u>**Zulu**</u>	African nation/tribe
2.	<u>**Ritz**</u>	prestigious hotel
3.	<u>**Arizona**</u>	state
4.	<u>**Zion**</u>	another name for Israel
5.	<u>**Liz**</u>	female nickname
6.	<u>**Tazo**</u>	Starbucks name brand tea
7.	<u>**Zen**</u>	branch of Buddhism
8.	<u>**wizard**</u>	magician
9.	<u>**klutz**</u>	clumsy
10.	<u>**fez**</u>	kind of hat
11.	<u>**blazer**</u>	kind of jacket
12.	<u>**size**</u>	measurement
13.	<u>**lizard**</u>	reptile
14.	<u>**maze**</u>	labyrinth
15.	<u>**zoo**</u>	habitat for animals
16.	<u>**Zodiac**</u>	horoscope

HOMEWORK 3:8, CARDINAL NUMBERS 30–60
Write the Number, p. 129

1. <u>32</u>	8. <u>57</u>	15. <u>63</u>
2. <u>66</u>	9. <u>48</u>	16. <u>46</u>
3. <u>61</u>	10. <u>53</u>	17. <u>37</u>
4. <u>40</u>	11. <u>44</u>	18. <u>58</u>
5. <u>49</u>	12. <u>60</u>	19. <u>59</u>
6. <u>45</u>	13. <u>34</u>	20. <u>41</u>
7. <u>36</u>	14. <u>42</u>	

HOMEWORK 3:11, "DOWN" LETTERS
Order the Words, p. 139

Names

<u>4</u> Paul	<u>3</u> Kyle	<u>6</u> Lynn
<u>2</u> Mary	<u>7</u> Yoon	
<u>5</u> Ryan	<u>1</u> Maya	

More Names

<u>1</u> Quinn	<u>3</u> Yolanda	<u>7</u> Peter
<u>4</u> Lydia	<u>2</u> Taylor	
<u>6</u> Priscilla	<u>5</u> Eveyln	

Places

<u>6</u> Quebec	<u>3</u> Sydney
<u>1</u> Quizno's	<u>5</u> Quiche shop
<u>2</u> Plaza	<u>4</u> Baker's Square

Things

<u>2</u> puppy	<u>4</u> plywood	<u>1</u> prize	<u>3</u> quartz

More Things

<u>1</u> map	<u>5</u> onyx	<u>4</u> yarn
<u>3</u> quilt	<u>2</u> yen	

Crossword Puzzle, p. 140

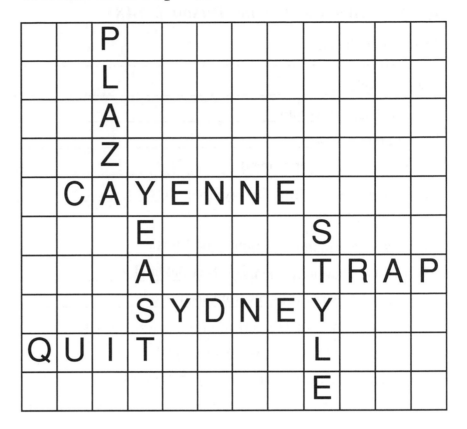

HOMEWORK 3:12, LENGTHS OF TIME
New Signs, p. 144–145

Minidialogue 3: <u>cookie; biscuit</u>

Minidialogue 4: <u>popcorn</u>

Minidialogue 7: <u>videophone (used by Deaf people to talk with each other)</u>

Minidialogue 8: <u>pretty; lovely; beautiful</u>

Minidialogues 6, 7 and 10: <u>longer than expected (timewise); a long time</u>

Minidialogue 10: <u>to remain in a place in readiness of or in anticipation of...</u>

HOMEWORK 3:13, CONVERSATION 4
Information about Another Person, p. 148

Narrative 1 (Isias)

Name: __Kyle__

Lives in (city): __Fremont__

Near/area: __N/A__

Type of residence: __apartment__   size: __medium-sized__

How long have they lived there (years?): __5 years__

Live with: __his wife__

Pets (type, how many): __1 rabbit and 1 turtle__

Work (place, how long – years?): __East Oakland__

How do they get to work: __by train and bus__

How long it takes to get to work from home: __45 minutes__

How do you get to class: __rides with a friend__

How long does it take to get to class: __15 minutes__

Narrative 2 (Priscilla)

Name: __April__

Lives in (city): __here at the college__

Near/area: __near the bookstore__

Type of residence: __dormitory__   size: __small__

How long have they lived there (years?): __two years__

Live with: __one roommate who grew up in England__

Pets (type, how many): __none at the dorm, but has one dog living with parents__

Work (place, how long – years?): __library__

How do they get to work: __by bicycle__

How long it takes to get to work from home: __8 minutes__

How do you get to class: __by bicycle__

How long does it take to get to class: __3 minutes__

UNIT 3 REVIEW: AUTOBIOGRAPHIES, *p. 154*

Autobiography 1 (narrated by Cinnie)

Name **Emma**

Personal information: Emma lives with her husband in a fairly large loft in South San Francisco. They've lived there 3 years. They have no pets. In the future, she wants to have a bird so she can teach it to speak.

Emma works in Fremont which takes takes 1 hour to get to by bus. She dislikes the long commute. Emma wants to find a job near where she lives because she does not have a car.

Remember Emma's favorite color is red. When you enter her house, one wall is painted red, the opposite wall is painted white. The ceiling is painted red with white dots. The wall facing you as you enter the house is orange. Her husband thinks she might be an oddball. Maybe she is.

She says it's time to go eat, then says goodbye.

Autobiography 2 (narrated by Stefanie)

Name **Sara**

Personal information: Sara has lived with her family 26 years. She is the only Deaf person in her family, but everyone in her family knows sign language. Sara likes to chat with her Deaf and hearing friends who sign. When she meets hearing people who do not sign, she writes notes with them, but she never speaks with her voice.

She works in a language lab, assisting students who want to come practice their ASL skills.

She goes to work on her blue motorcycle—remember her favorite color is blue.

Now, Sara is learning how to knit. She knitted a pink coat that she gave to her mother. Her mother likes it.

Her girlfriend has arrived to come pick her up to go see a movie. She says she'll see you later.

Autobiography 3 (narrated by Tyrone)

Name **Billy**

Personal information: Billy has two dogs which he takes to a park to play frisbee. After they get tired fetching frisbee, he takes them home.

Billy lives in a small house by a train station. He usually takes the train to the college where he works. It takes 20 minutes to get there from home.

Billy likes country western dancing. He gets to wear boots, blue jeans, a red and white plaid shirt, a scarf around his neck and a cowboy hat.

Billy also likes eating chocolate candy. Sara, knowing he likes chocolate, always gives him pieces of chocolate candy.

Billy has to stop talking because Emma is hungry and wants the two of them to go out to eat now.

UNIT 4 ANSWER KEYS

HOMEWORK 4:2, NEGATIVE RESPONSES
Check the Response, p. 182

1.	✔	
2.	✔	
3.		✔
4.	✔	
5.		✔
6.		✔
7.		✔
8.	✔	
9.		✔
10.	✔	

HOMEWORK 4:3, ROCKING NUMBERS
Circle the Number, p. 185

1.	68	(78)	6.	87	(97)
2.	69	(89)	7.	(79)	89
3.	76	(86)	8.	(98)	87
4.	86	(87)	9.	(69)	97
5.	(67)	78	10.	(68)	86

HOMEWORK 4:7, TELLING AGES
Identify Number Type, p. 198

age

1. ___7___ (age) cardinal
2. ___18___ (age) cardinal
3. ___20___ age (cardinal)
4. ___6___ age (cardinal)
5. ___13___ (age) cardinal
6. ___45___ age (cardinal)
7. ___24___ (age) cardinal
8. ___78___ age (cardinal)
9. ___92___ (age) cardinal
10. ___16___ (age) cardinal
11. ___21___ (age) cardinal
12. ___82___ age (cardinal)
13. ___15___ (age) cardinal
14. ___60___ age (cardinal)
15. ___99___ (age) cardinal
16. ___3___ (age) cardinal
17. ___19___ age (cardinal)
18. ___48___ age (cardinal)
19. ___23___ age (cardinal)
20. ___10___ (age) cardinal

HOMEWORK 4:11, TEN YEARS LATER... *p. 205*

(**woman reading letter**) Fell in love with a nice looking doctor. They dated for 2 years. They are now engaged and plan to wed next June.

(**woman stirring bowl**) She had been married for 32 years. She and her husband fell out of love, and got a divorce. Since she is close to her daughter, she moved in with her (woman reading letter).

(**man reading newspaper**) Single, not married. Went to France where he met a woman whose husband had passed way. She has two children who are twins. The man married the woman. Now he has two stepchildren. How interesting!

(**pregnant woman & kissing man**) They gave birth to a boy who is Deaf and is now 9 years old. He attends a school for the Deaf. The parents have been learning ASL. They plan to adopt a Deaf girl. They are now looking for a house.

(**little girl**) She is now 13 years old. Attends Junior High School. There she met a boy who she discovered was her half brother. How did it happen? Her father dated the boy's mother many years ago, and she became pregnant with his baby.

(**cat**) The cat gave birth to two kittens, one has a black fur and a white nose, and the other has an orange fur with brown stripes. The family is searching for a new home for the kittens.

HOMEWORK 4:12, REVIEWING NUMBERS 1–100
What Number Is It?, p. 206

1.	68	10.	2	19.	87
2.	61	11.	62	20.	70
3.	14	12.	91	21.	22
4.	99	13.	27	22.	37
5.	5	14.	56	23.	81
6.	39	15.	28	24.	53
7.	35	16.	78	25.	42
8.	80	17.	11	26.	31
9.	19	18.	65	27.	82

HOMEWORK 4:14, COMMENTING ON FAMILY MEMBERS
Autobiographies, p. 213–214

Autobiography 1

Name **Emma**

Personal information: Emma's parents are Deaf. She has two brothers and two sisters. She is the 4th child. They all can hear and are good signers. The oldest, 2nd to the oldest and the youngest siblings never married. The third oldest (her brother) married and divorced twice and is now engaged. He has two sons.

Emma has been married 25 years. She has two children, a girl who is now 24 years old and a boy who is 19. Her daughter is away at college. She and her girlfriends are going to tour England on bicycles for three months. Her son is now in college. Since he was a boy, he has liked playing computer games. Whenever they (Emma and son) play games together, he always wins. He's very good! Now that all the children have left the nest, she and her husband are the only ones in the house. She thinks she might get a dog and teach it signs. (not a bird that she had thought about getting).

She thanks the audience for listening to her family story and says she will see you later.

Autobiography 2

Name <u>Sara</u>

Personal information: Sara is the only one in her family who is Deaf. She has one sister and two brothers. She is the youngest child.

Her oldest sister is 30 years old. She has a boyfriend she's been dating for seven years. He hasn't yet proposed marriage. She is still waiting.

Her two brothers are twins. They are 28 years old. The older brother is married and has a 6-month old daughter. She is cute! The other twin brother is gay. He has a partner who writes children's books. The brother himself is a doctor. They adopted a 4 year old boy.

Sarah is 26 years old. She is a graduate of Gallaudet University. She works at a language lab. She enjoys working with ASL students.

When she was 15 years old, her parents quarreled constantly and didn't get along, then they got a divorce. When she was 21 years old, both parents reconciled and married again. They're still together which is good.

Some of her favorite activities are riding a motorcycle through the hills (remember she has a blue motorcycle), backpacking, hiking and bird watching.

She checks the clock and says she has a lot of student papers to correct, so she has to go now.

Autobiography 3

Name <u>Billy</u>

Personal information: Billy's parents are Deaf. He has a sister who is also Deaf. She is married. She and her husband adopted a girl who is now 6 years old and Deaf. Her name is Lynn.

Billy has been dating a woman for 3 years. They may get married in the near future. Her name is Amy. She is Deaf but her parents are not.

In his family, there are many relatives who are Deaf. He has three aunts and two uncles who are Deaf. He also has four Deaf cousins and 3 cousins who are not. They all know sign language.

One of his two dogs is deaf and understands and responds to some signs...like "eat," "sit," "walk," and "toilet." It's a good dog.

He checks his watch and says he has to go bowling now.

HOMEWORK 5:8, "OUT OF THE ORDINARY" ACTIVITY
Circle the Day, Part of the Day, p. 268

1.   DAY

S	M	T	W	T	F	S
4	5	6	7	8	9	10
11	12	13	**14**	15	16	17
18	19	20	21	22	23	24

PART OF DAY: AM   PM   **EVE**

2.   DAY

S	M	T	W	T	F	S
4	5	6	7	8	9	10
11	12	13	**14**	15	16	17
18	19	20	21	22	23	24

PART OF DAY: **AM**   PM   EVE

3.   DAY

S	M	T	W	T	F	S
4	5	6	7	8	9	10
11	12	13	**14**	**15**	16	17
18	19	20	21	22	23	24

PART OF DAY: AM   **PM**   EVE

4.   DAY

S	M	T	W	T	F	S
4	5	6	7	8	9	10
11	12	13	**14**	15	16	17
18	19	20	21	22	**23**	24

PART OF DAY: **AM   PM   EVE**

5.   DAY

S	M	T	W	T	F	S
4	**5**	6	7	8	9	10
11	12	13	**14**	15	16	17
18	19	20	21	22	23	24

PART OF DAY: AM   PM   **EVE**

6.   DAY

S	M	T	W	T	F	S
4	5	6	7	8	9	10
11	12	13	**14**	15	16	17
18	19	20	21	**22**	23	24

PART OF DAY: AM   **PM**   EVE

7.   DAY

S	M	T	W	T	F	S
4	5	**6**	7	8	9	10
11	12	13	**14**	15	16	17
18	19	20	21	22	23	24

PART OF DAY: AM   **PM**   EVE

8.   DAY

S	M	T	W	T	F	S
4	5	6	7	8	9	10
11	12	13	**14**	15	16	17
18	19	20	**21**	22	23	24

PART OF DAY: **AM**   PM   EVE

9.   DAY

S	M	T	W	T	F	S
4	5	6	7	8	9	10
11	12	**13**	**14**	15	16	17
18	19	20	21	22	23	24

PART OF DAY: AM   PM   **EVE**

10.   DAY

S	M	T	W	T	F	S
4	5	6	7	8	9	10
11	12	13	**14**	15	16	**17**
18	19	20	21	22	23	24

PART OF DAY: **AM   PM   EVE**

11.   DAY

S	M	T	W	T	F	S
4	5	6	7	8	9	10
11	12	13	**14**	15	16	17
18	19	20	21	22	23	24

PART OF DAY: AM   **PM**   EVE

12.   DAY

S	M	T	W	T	F	S
4	5	6	7	8	9	10
11	12	13	**14**	15	16	17
18	19	20	**21**	22	23	24

PART OF DAY: AM   **PM**   EVE

HOMEWORK 5:8, "OUT OF THE ORDINARY" ACTIVITY
Test Yourself, p. 272

1.

18-31
_____

2.

8-14
_____

3.

22-28
_____

4.

1-14
_____

HOMEWORK 5:8, COMMONLY FINGERSPELLED WORDS
Write the Word 1, page 274

1. COUCH

2. VEST

3. SIZE

4. PUPPY

5. QUILT

6. TEE

7. X-RAY

8. PRIZE

9. JUNK

10. GIFT

11. BAG

12. BILLS

HOMEWORK 5:8, COMMONLY FINGERSPELLED WORDS
Write the Word 2, p. 275

1. TV	5. ZOO	9. DESK	13. CONDO
2. HAM	6. FAX	10. TWIN	14. JUICE
3. ICE	7. VAN	11. HERB	15. BURRITO
4. GAS	8. BBQ	12. TRUCK	16. PLASTIC

UNIT 5 REVIEW, AUTOBIOGRAPHIES, *p. 279*

Autobiography 1
Name **Emma**

Personal information: Last Friday morning Emma's sister wanted her to go clothes shopping. They shopped all day. When Emma arrived home, she was too tired to cook so she ordered out. Her husband picked up the food and the two of them ate dinner.

Saturday was beautiful. The sun was shining. In the morning, Emma sat outside and read the papers. In the afternoon, while watering the lawn, she saw something crawling in thegrass. It was a turtle. She went door to door to try and find its owner. No luck! So she brought it home and put it in a box.

In the evening, she and her husband went to watch their nephew play basketball. It was a good game. And it was fun for them.

Sunday morning, Emma's parents and her husband went to a Deaf church. In the afternoon, she and her sister hosted a party for their aunt and uncle who are going to live in Mexico for 1 year. Her uncle is a banker. On the weekends, the two of them plan to travel around and sight-see. In 6 months, Emma and her sister hope to join their aunt and uncle in Mexico and see some of the sights. Emma asks if you (the audience) know what turtles eat. She is going to the pet store to find out.

Autobiography 2

Name **Billy**

Personal information: Billy is tired. Yesterday he stayed home vacuuming the floors, and cleaning outside (in the yard), and repairing and repainting the old fence.

This morning, he went to the dentist to have his teeth cleaned and then in the afternoon he helped his friend pack boxes and move to a new house.

Tonight, his girlfriend is coming over, and he is going to cook a Mexican dish. He crosses his fingers it will all turn out well.

Tomorrow, he is going to an all-day class on Mexican dancing.

Next Saturday, his ASL class from college is going to an amusement park. They will be trying out some new rides (roller coasters) and practicing signing all day. There are 18 girls and 6 boys in his class.

Next Sunday, he plans to stay home and watch movies.

He says he is tired and needs to go take a nap now.

Autobiography 3

Name **Sarah**

Personal information: Remember I told you about my brother's partner who writes children's books? Well, he asked if I could draw pictures for his book. Since I am working in a language lab, I've learned how to do graphics on the computer. I will certainly help out.

All day last Saturday, I drew a picture of a bird sitting in a tree. The bird is red all over with a yellow beak. In the back of the picture are hills with rabbits hopping around. On the bottom of the picture is a house where a rat lives with its family. But I didn't like the picture so I threw it away. I will draw a new one next Wednesday.

Last Saturday night, my brother and his partner went to a party so I babysat their son (my nephew). We played a game (checkers), and sat together reading a book. Eventually, he felt asleep. So cute! I really enjoyed babysitting him.

Last Sunday morning, my sister, my friend Judy, and Billy's girlfriend and I went to a zoo. After watching the animals, I started thinking about volunteering at the zoo and help feed the animals.

Later in the afternoon, I stopped at a gas station to fill the tank and then drove home.

I really had a nice weekend. I enjoyed telling you what happened. Hope to see you again soon! Bye-bye.

SIGNING NATURALLY

Topic Index